Car-Free® in Cleveland

The Guide to Public Transit and Transportation Alternatives in Greater Cleveland
1st Edition, 2000

Researched and written by the Alt-Trans Cleveland project:
Greg Aliberti, Brad Flamm, Bill Hinkley, Michael Lewyn,
Karen Lippmann, Mike McGraw, Ryan McKenzie,
Kim Palmer and Ken Prendergast

Cover art by Jeff Suntala

EcoCity Cleveland
Special Publication

For additional copies, send $9.00 per copy ($6.95 plus $2.05 to cover sales tax,
postage and handling) in a check or money order to
EcoCity Cleveland,
2841 Scarborough Road,
Cleveland Heights, OH 44118
For inquiries about bulk discounts, call 216-932-3007.

PARTICIPANTS

Alt-Trans Cleveland is a project that works for livable communities by promoting transportation alternatives and providing information about transportation choices in the Greater Cleveland metropolitan area. The project is facilitated by EcoCity Cleveland, a nonprofit environmental planning organization. For more information, contact EcoCity Cleveland at 2841 Scarborough Rd., Cleveland Heights, OH 44118, phone: 216-932-3007, e-mail: ecomail@ecocleveland.org, Web site: www.ecocleveland.org. For membership information, see p. 102.

ACKNOWLEDGMENTS

The members of Alt-Trans Cleveland put in long hours, many as volunteers, to make this book a success. Michael Lewyn wrote the first draft in 1997. Ken Prendergast and Karen Lippmann expanded, revised and updated the text. Kim Palmer contributed design and desktop publishing skills. Greg Aliberti created a logo, took photos and helped with the graphic look of the book. Brad Flamm, Mike McGraw and Ryan McKenzie helped with research, writing and editing. Abe Bruckman, Martha Loughridge, Chris Ronayne, John Seydlitz and Esther Wyss contributed additional comments and advice.

Special thanks to The George Gund Foundation for providing the funding needed to get this project off the ground. And thanks also to the following people and organizations for their valuable contributions: David Beach, the director of EcoCity Cleveland, who provided editorial guidance and administered the project; RoseMary Covington, Joel Freilich, Steve Bitto and Richard Enty of Greater Cleveland RTA for their advice, ideas and early support of the effort; Mary Reed, who put in long hours to write a successful grant proposal; the Greater Cleveland Convention and Visitors Bureau for allowing us to use several photographs; and Jeff Suntala, who created the cover art for this first edition of *Car-Free in Cleveland*.

Copyright © 2000
EcoCity Cleveland
All rights reserved

The "Car-Free®" name is a trademark of the Association for Public Transportation, Inc., P.O. Box 192, Cambridge, MA 02238. Registered U.S. Patent & Trademark Office. All rights reserved.

ISBN 0-9663999-1-9

TABLE OF CONTENTS

QUICK GUIDE TO IMPORTANT PHONE NUMBERS ....INSIDE FRONT COVER

CHAPTER ONE: INTRODUCTION..1

CHAPTER TWO: THE GREATER CLEVELAND REGIONAL TRANSIT AUTHORITY 5

CHAPTER THREE: OTHER TRANSIT AGENCIES 17

CHAPTER FOUR: BICYCLES 27

CHAPTER FIVE: MORE TRANSPORTATION CHOICES 37

CHAPTER SIX: BEYOND CLEVELAND 45

CHAPTER SEVEN: PLACES TO SEE & THINGS TO DO..........57

CHAPTER EIGHT: GREATER CLEVELAND RTA BUS & RAPID ROUTES 88

III

INTRODUCTION

Tell native Clevelanders that you bought a book called *Car-Free in Cleveland* and you might hear a surprised laugh. "That's ridiculous," they'll say. "You can't get around Cleveland without a car!"

To be sure, the Cleveland area is not often viewed as a paradise for transit riders, cyclists, and pedestrians. What Cleveland lacks in reputation, however, it more than makes up in choices. This book is about those choices – the alternative ways you have to get around our city and its environs without a car.

What do you mean, "car-free?"

First things first: Car-free doesn't necessarily mean car-less, at least not all the time. Automobiles can be a useful way to get around. And occasionally, there's just no substitute for them.

But your horizons don't have to be defined by whether you have a car. You have many great ways to get where you're going without having to drive yourself, by yourself. You can move from Point A to Point B comfortably, inexpensively and conveniently via buses (locals, expresses, freeway flyers, intercities, para-transit and community circulators), trains (the Rapid and Amtrak), taxis, bicycles (on city streets, bike paths, bike lanes, bike routes, or bikeways), water taxis, planes, carpools, van-pools, or just by strolling or power-walking to your destination.

> **BY THE WAY**
>
> If the RTA's buses and trains disappeared permanently, nearly 250 miles of new urban freeway lanes would have to be built to make up for their loss.

This book expands your transportation horizons by helping you think in new ways about how to get around.

Many Clevelanders already live a car-free lifestyle – either by choice or by circumstance. More would love to be car-free more of the time. Whatever your situation, this book gives you all the information you'll need to be car-free, whether for a day or for a lifetime.

Why car-free?

A car-free lifestyle can be a better lifestyle – not just for those who live it, but for everybody in Greater Cleveland. How we choose to move influences the shape of our own lives each day, as well as the quality of our neighborhoods and region. For example, walking and cycling combine transportation with exercise, while contributing to a cleaner, quieter city environment. Besides, worrying about breakdowns, break-ins, traffic jams, parking problems, expensive repairs, and road rage doesn't have to be an unavoidable evil of living in cities the size of Cleveland. Why not consider a few ways to simplify your life, demonstrate care for your community, benefit from a lower-mileage, lower-stress lifestyle, and save some serious cash in the process?

That high-mileage life sure isn't cheap, if you think about how much owning and operating a car costs. According to the American Automobile Association, the average cost for owning and operating a new car is approximately $6,400 every year. And don't forget the billions of dollars we all pay in taxes every year to subsidize the infrastructure of the car culture. Being car-free means you can pocket some of that money for yourself. What would you do with an extra few thousand bucks a year?

Choices, choices, choices

There's no question that trying new things can be challenging. Many of us aren't really sure what transportation options are available out there. When using new ways to get around, we're uncertain about how to make plans for ourselves and with others.

But, whether it's an everyday commute, an evening out with friends, or a spontaneous weekend getaway, *Car-Free in Cleveland* does much of the leg-work for you. Schedules, maps, and phone numbers are all here to help you plan your travels. We've included the most up-to-date information. (However, If you come across an old disconnected phone number or bus route that has changed, please let us know.)

Public transit is an obvious car-free alternative, and Greater Cleveland has many extensive, interconnected bus and rail transit systems. You'll find an outline of those systems here, along with detailed background information about them.

Beyond the bus and Rapid rail systems, *Car-Free in Cleveland* profiles bicycling, walking, car-pooling, van-pooling, taxicabs, and car rental as possible local options. For longer trips, you'll also get the scoop on airline, rail, and intercity bus services in the pages that follow.

> **CONTACT ALT-TRANS CLEVELAND AT:**
>
> c/o Eco City Cleveland
> 2841 Scarborough Road
> Cleveland Heights, OH 44118
> ☎ 216-932-3007
> FAX: 216-932-6069
> ecomail@ecocleveland.org

Give it a try!

Car-Free in Cleveland invites you to explore Northeast Ohio with transit, by bicycle, on foot, and via any other creative option you can dream up. Just think – you'll enjoy the freedom of not looking for a parking space, not having to pump gas on cold, rainy days, and not fighting traffic and road-rage crazies. Sit back, relax, and imagine the possibilities. *Car-Free in Cleveland* can take you there. You have all the information you need in your hands. Now read on and see how easy it really is!

Greater Cleveland RTA

Courtesy of David Beach

THE GREATER CLEVELAND REGIONAL TRANSIT AUTHORITY

Living car-free doesn't mean you don't get out and about. You're as busy as anyone else, and you have places to go. But living car-free does mean that when you go to work, school, shopping, out on the town, or to visit your parents you leave the driving (and the parking headaches, the traffic jams, the gas station pit stops and all the other joys of a car-full life) to somebody else. And that means that public transit is often just the ticket!

Car-Free in Cleveland

The bottom line

The bottom line is this: leading a car-free lifestyle helps your bottom line. Not your tush, we're talking money here. Consider for a minute that the American Automobile Association estimates the average new car costs about $6,400 a year to own and operate.

That's right, once you send in the monthly payment check, buy gas and oil, pay for insurance, shell out for parking and registration and E-checks (and maybe even an occasional ticket when the meter runs fast), and then factor in long-term maintenance costs, you'll spend over $525 a month for the privilege of a shiny new car! Even older cars, the ones that many families keep as a second (or sometimes third) car, will cost thousands of dollars per year.

So living a more car-free lifestyle pays off in a big way. One recent study found that giving up a second car can save a family as much as $4,300 a year.

Now, that's not all extra spending money, of course, because you'll still have other transportation expenses. First, you'll need to spend $600 a year on transit, the cost of an annual RTA express-fare pass. You might also ⇩

Fortunately, getting around on transit systems can be easy, affordable, and convenient. But you've got to know the system, and that's what this section of *Car-Free in Cleveland* is all about. From routes and schedules to fares and transfers, we'll give you the lowdown on the Greater Cleveland RTA. In the following chapter, we'll give you all the details for the other transit agencies that you'll want to use when exploring the rest of our region.

We cover the basics here and give you some lesser-known hints and tips about using public transit. For information we can't cover here, just give the transit agencies a call. They all have helpful customer service and scheduling info lines.

The RTA

With over 100 bus routes, four rapid transit rail lines, and 365-days-a-year operations, your most accessible choice for getting around car-free in Northeast Ohio is the Greater Cleveland Regional Transit Authority (RTA). The RTA system serves more than 60 million riders each year, covers all of Cuyahoga County and conveniently connects with other county and municipal public transit systems operating in the region (not to mention Cleveland Hopkins International Airport, Amtrak inter-city train service and Greyhound inter-city buses). The system's main hub is located in downtown Cleveland

6

at Tower City Center, on Public Square. Other hubs are located east, west and south of the city.

RTA's bus system

There are three main types of RTA bus routes: Local buses, Express/Flyer buses, and the Community Circulators and downtown Loop buses.

Local buses provide extensive service throughout the City of Cleveland and other Cuyahoga County communities and cost just $1.25 a ride. They circulate on the major avenues and boulevards ("trunk routes" as they're called in transit agency lingo) and on some smaller streets, too, connecting Cleveland neighborhoods and many suburbs. You'll generally use the Local buses for shorter trips, because stops are placed closely together (sometimes every two to three blocks). At busy times of the day, the bus may drop riders off or pick new riders up at every single stop. Intervals between Local buses may be as short as just a few minutes during peak-travel hours. RTA's #6 bus, for example, has the highest ridership of all of RTA's routes and provides service every six minutes during the day up and down Euclid Avenue between Public Square and East Cleveland. In addition, most late-night service is provided by local buses.

Express and Flyer buses provide longer-distance travel with fewer stops, generally connecting Cleveland's suburbs with downtown. The cost per ride is $1.50. Express buses (designated by an "X" following the

The bottom line

rack up $300 a year on taxi fare for when you go shopping for bulkier items or need to get home late at night. Another $400 a year will pay to occasionally rent a car when you want to take a fun weekend trip or you need the carrying capacity of a private car.

That adds up to just $1,300, and you're left with $3,000 in savings!

To most of us, $3,000 is a pretty good amount of money. You can rent an apartment that costs $250 more a month, for example. Or sock it away in your savings. Or take a trip, see more movies and concerts, buy a lot of great books, nicer clothes or contribute to more good causes.

But that's not all. There's an improved bottom line for everybody else too. When you save money by living a more car-free life, you also reduce congestion on the roads, help improve air and water quality by cutting down on pollution, do your bit to reduce greenhouse gases that are raising the earth's temperature, and decrease our dependence on oil as a fuel source.

Any way you slice it, a car-free lifestyle's a good deal for everybody!

Car-Free in Cleveland

route number) usually run all day. Flyer buses get their name because they "fly" along the interstates, usually serving commuters only during morning and afternoon rush hours (designated by an "F" following the route number).

Stops along the Express and Flyer routes are less frequent than on Local bus routes, so check the route schedules for details, or, when in doubt, ask the driver.

Community Circulators & Loop buses: Community Circulator buses operate set circular routes within neighborhoods, such as in Tremont, St. Clair-Superior, and the Lee-Miles areas (they're numbered 801, 802, 803, etc.). They're inexpensive rides, costing just 50¢, and they link people's homes and apartments with local shopping, services, medical facilities and RTA's local and express buses. You can board a community circulator at any regular RTA bus stop or – and this is unique for RTA buses – you can flag the driver to stop anywhere for you along the route.

> **BY THE WAY**
>
> By a wide margin, Greater Cleveland is Ohio's most transit-oriented metropolitan area, with more than 60 million mass transit rides per year. In fact, only 13 other big cities in the U.S. use their public transit systems more than we do in Greater Cleveland. Ranking second in Ohio is Greater Cincinnati, which generates just half as many transit trips per year.

The Loop buses, also just 50¢ a ride, circle through Cleveland's downtown area every few minutes from 6 a.m. to 6 p.m. weekdays. There are two routes – the #147 City Center Loop and the #247 Outer Loop – that link just about all downtown destinations. Be aware, however, that Loop routes can sometimes be confusing, even to seasoned local transit users. Check out the downtown map on pages 106-107, and don't hesitate to stop and ask drivers if they're going your way.

RTA's Rapid system

New Yorkers get around on the subway, Boston's got the "T," San Francisco has "BART," and Clevelanders ride the "Rapid." RTA's train service is Ohio's only rail-based public transit service, operating on the Red, Blue, Green and Waterfront lines. Tower City on Public Square is the rail system's hub, providing access to all of the lines and permitting easy transfers from one to the other, and to many RTA bus routes.

The Red Line travels from Cleveland Hopkins International Airport through West Side neighborhoods to the Tower City downtown station and then eastward to the Louis Stokes/Windermere Station in East Cleveland. It differs from the other Rapid lines in that it's a heavy-rail system with larger cars that are boarded from raised platforms inside Red Line stations.

The Green and Blue lines connect downtown Cleveland's waterfront attractions and Tower City Center to Shaker Square on the eastern edge of the city. They then split, continuing to the east into Shaker Heights. The Green Line follows Shaker Boulevard due east from Shaker Square and teminates at Green Road. The Blue Line cuts southeast at Shaker Square, follows Van Aken Boulevard, terminating at Warrensville Center and Chagrin roads.

> **BY THE WAY**
>
> In 1968, Cleveland was the first city in the Western Hemisphere to link its downtown and international airport with a rail transit line. The Greater Cleveland Regional Transit Authority's Red Line airport station, located inside the air terminal, was completely modernized in 1994.

Trains that run on the Green and Blue lines are light-rail cars which load from low-level platforms. Since the Green and Blue lines are combined with the Red Line between Tower City Center, East 34th St./Campus and East 55th St. stations, these three facilities each have high-level and low-level platforms. Cleveland's rail system is the only one in the nation which has these dual-platform stations.

The Waterfront Line is a westerly continuation of the Green/Blue Rapid lines starting from Tower City. The route takes riders through the Flats entertainment district and past North Coast Harbor destinations, making very easy connections with popular

Car-Free in Cleveland

tourist spots such as the Rock and Roll Hall of Fame, Great Lakes Science Center and the Steamship William G. Mather Museum.

Rapid schedules: Rapid trains run every 6-24 minutes on weekdays, and every 15-30 minutes on weekends and holidays. First trains run on the Red Line at 3:39 a.m. westbound and 4:32 a.m. eastbound; on the Blue Line at about 4:30 a.m.; and on the Green Line at 5:55 a.m. Last trains run on the Red Line at 10 p.m., and on the Blue/Green/ Waterfront lines at about 12 midnight (a shuttle bus continues Red Line service on the West side between the airport and Tower City between 10 p.m. and 1 a.m. only). If there is an evening sporting event downtown the last trains will leave Tower City no earlier than 90 minutes after the end of the game, even if it goes into overtime. During summer weekends only, Rapid service to 2 a.m. is available (see special services, events and routes in the next section).

Special services, events and routes

RTA runs several routes to serve regional attractions and special events. For example, several Flyer Service routes have been established to shuttle Cleveland sports fans directly from suburban Park-n-Ride lots to Jacobs Field and Cleveland Browns Stadium. Costing $1.50 each way, these buses depart one hour before game time from eight locations: Brecksville Municipal Parking, Euclid Park-n-Ride, Great Northern Shopping Center, Parmatown Mall, Solon Square Shopping Center, Southgate USA, Strongsville Park-n-Ride and the Westlake Park-n-Ride. Immediately following a game's end, riders board the buses for the return trip (see Laketran section for Lake County Gateway buses).

Rail service on the Red, Blue, Green, and Waterfront lines offers extended evening hours on Fridays and Saturdays, from Memorial Day to Labor Day. This is available for people staying downtown late to enjoy a night on the town. The last trains leave downtown for the suburbs at 2 a.m.

Another special service is the #441 bus route connecting the Van Aken/Blue Line Rapid station, Randall Park Mall, and Southgate USA with Geauga Lake Amusement Park and Sea World. In service only when the parks are open (roughly Memorial Day through Labor Day), the #441 buses run every 30 minutes from about 7 a.m. to 11:30 p.m.

Greater Cleveland RTA

Call the RTA Answerline (216-621-9500) for details about these and other special services. Also, watch for notices about discounts to many special events at Gund Arena and elsewhere that are available when you present an RTA transfer card at the box office.

Paratransit

Although many of RTA's regular bus services are equipped with lifts for the disabled, a special ADA (Americans with Disabilities Act) Complementary Paratransit Service is also available. Paratransit service is available Monday through Thursday from 6 a.m. to 10 p.m., Friday and Saturday from 6 a.m. to 11 p.m., and Sunday from 8 a.m. to 10 p.m. You must apply for ADA certification through the RTA offices, then call ahead to schedule your trip.

Transit centers

Transit centers are beginning to appear where several bus routes and/or Rapid lines come together so that riders can transfer with greater ease. These centers offer a landscaped plaza, heated/cooled waiting room, and pay phones. Centers are now at Parmatown Mall in Parma, west of Westgate Mall in Fairview Park, and downtown Cleveland at Tower City Center. Plans are currently in the works for many more.

RTA fares

RTA fares can be paid with cash (remember, exact change only!) or with a variety of RTA tickets and passes, including day passes, express passes, family passes and transfers.

Normally you pay your fare or present your pass or transfer to the

RTA FARES

	LOCAL	EXPRESS
Cash (one trip)	$1.25	$1.50
Day pass	$4.00	$4.00
Family day pass (1 adult and up to 3 children)	$6.00	$6.00
Weekly pass	$11.25	$13.50
Monthly pass	$45.00	$54.00
Annual pass	$495.00	$594.00
Weekly Off-Peak Pass	$7.50	$7.50
Tickets in advance (1, 2, 5 or 10)	$1.19 each	$1.43 each

Car-Free in Cleveland

How to board a bus

There are a few more things you need to keep in mind when you're getting ready for that ride on an RTA bus:

Exact change: If you're paying with cash, you have to have the exact fare, because bus drivers can't make change. Fortunately, exact fare doesn't have to be paid in coins, because coins and dollar bills are accepted in the fare box you'll find at the front of any RTA bus.

Using passes: If you've bought a ticket or RTA pass in advance, simply show it to the bus driver when you board the bus.

Local vs. Express: You have to know if you'll be paying the fare for a Local bus or an Express/Flyer bus. If it's a Local, have $1.25 ready. If it's an Express or Flyer, have $1.50. And if you're transferring from a Local to an Express/Flyer bus, you'll need to pay an additional 25¢.

Transfers: You need to know if your trip is going to be on a single bus or if you'll need to switch to another bus to get to your destination. It's no problem, and no extra money, to transfer to another bus, but you do have to RTA bus operator when you first board a bus, though there are exceptions to this rule. On the Rapid system, you pay your fare or present your pass at a turnstile when you enter a station or to the train driver when you board the train, depending upon which station you use to board the train. If you're not sure about when or how to pay, just ask the bus driver or Rapid operator.

Tickets and passes are available at the RTA Customer Service Center, 315 Euclid Avenue, and at over 180 participating banks and retail stores around town. Look for the "RTA Passes Sold Here" logo in the window, or call the RTA Answerline at 216-621-9500 for the nearest outlet. See the chart on page 11 for prices.

Day pass: Allows unlimited travel from the time of first use until 3 a.m. the next day on all services within Cuyahoga County. Day passes are available only at RTA's Customer Service Center (315 Euclid Avenue), RTA's Tower City Rapid station (open rush hours only), and at RTA's Hopkins Airport Rapid station.

Family day pass: Allows one day of unlimited rides on all services for one adult and up to three children, ages 6-15, from the time of first use until 3 a.m. the next day on all services within Cuyahoga County. Its effective date is the same as the regular day pass.

The passes described below are sold in both local and express versions.

Express passes are valid for all services. If you buy a local pass, then need to use or transfer to an express or flyer bus or one of the Rapid system's rail lines, you will have to pay an extra 25¢.

Greater Cleveland RTA

Weekly pass: Allows unlimited travel from the time of first use to the following Sunday at midnight.

Monthly pass: Allows unlimited travel until midnight on the last day of the month.

Annual pass: For the year-round RTA user, this is a bargain, because you pay for the equivalent of 11 months of RTA service, but get to ride for 12 full months. Go anywhere, any route, anytime with this pass that is valid until midnight on Dec. 31 of the year you purchase it.

Weekly off-peak pass: Unlimited off-peak travel from Monday to the following Sunday at midnight. This is a great deal if you can avoid travel during RTA's peak hours (6 a.m. to 9 a.m. and 3 p.m. to 6 p.m., Monday through Friday). You can still use the pass during peak hours, if you need to, but the trip will cost an extra quarter.

Farecards of one, two, five and ten rides can also be purchased, if you'd like to save a little money by paying in advance.

Transfers

To get where you're going, you'll sometimes need to take more than one bus or Rapid. If you're not using a pass that allows unlimited rides, be sure to ask your driver for a transfer when paying your fare. Transfers are free, and can be used to make up to three connections, including bus-to-train transfers. If you're using a transfer to connect from a local route to an express route or a Rapid, you'll have to pay the 25¢ price difference.

Transfers are valid for two hours from issuance, and are good for any direction

How to board a bus

ask the bus driver for a transfer card when you're paying the fare.

When to pay: You have to know when to pay. In most cases, it's simple: you pay at the time you get on the bus. But on buses that provide both Local and Express service, you'll pay either $1.25 or $1.50, depending upon how long you stay on the bus. The bus driver won't know how long you intend to ride until you actually get off, so that's when you pay.

Exiting: You have to know where you can exit the bus. Usually, you can exit by either the front or rear doors. But if you're on one of those buses that do the Local and Express/Flyer thing, you can only get out by the front door because that's where you're going to pay the fare.

Asking questions: Finally, you have to remember that you don't have to remember all of this. When in doubt, just ask the bus driver. He or she should be happy to answer your question. RTA's motto is "Quality service to every customer, every day," and answering customer questions accurately is part of that commitment.

Car-Free in Cleveland

except for returning on the same route. (In other words, the only extra riding you can't do with a transfer is to take a round-trip on the same bus route or Rapid line.) When you get on the next bus, put your transfer in the slot of the fare box, just like you would use any pass card or pre-paid ticket.

With a transfer, you can even get off the bus or train on the way to your final destination, then get back on and continue in the original direction without paying again, as long as the transfer hasn't expired (expiration time is printed on the transfer). For instance, you can catch a bus heading toward downtown, hop off along the way to do some banking or get some breakfast, then take the next bus to resume your trip without paying another fare.

Hours of operation

RTA trip frequencies vary widely according to the route, the time of the day, the day of the week, and sometimes even according to season of the year. Basic RTA services run from early in the morning (around 6 a.m.) to early at night (about 9 p.m.). So if you want to get to work early or leave the office late, catch a 7 a.m. airplane, go see an early evening movie, or visit friends on your way home from school, you probably won't be stranded.

SPECIAL RTA FARES

Combination tickets (5)	$2.50
Senior and disabled (with RTA ID)	$.50
Student ticket	$1.00
(K-12, must be purchased through school)	
Downtown Loops (buses 147 and 247)	$0.50
Community Circulators (buses 801 to 808)	$0.50
Community Responsive Transit (paratransit)	$1.25
Trips from outside Cuyahoga County into Cuyahoga County	$2.50
Trips wholly outside Cuyahoga County	$1.50
Waterfront Line pass	$1.50
(good for unlimited rides for 4 hours)	

In some cases, there are even bus routes providing "night owl" service around-the-clock from Monday through Saturday. So if you've got a graveyard work shift or you just want to close your favorite pub, RTA will meet your needs. On the other hand, some routes, such as many of the express and flyer suburban commuter routes, may have as few as two or three buses a day and only during rush hours.

Greater Cleveland RTA

For more information, check out the summaries of RTA bus route and Rapid line services in the back of this book (the times and route information are current as of Fall 1999). If you want confirmation that the bus you need will be running when you want it (particularly if you're traveling early in the morning or late at night), call the RTA Answerline at 216-621-9500. The Answerline is a 24-hour, automated system, with operators available during the daytime until 6 p.m. Or check out RTA's Internet Web site to download current route schedules.

RTA CONTACT INFO

Answerline: 216-621-9500
Senior & ADA, 216-566-5285, ADA info 216-566-5124
Paratransit 216-781-1110, TDD 216-781-6148
TDD: 216-781-4271
1240 West 6th St., Cleveland, OH 44113
little.nhlink.net/~rta

Top ten car-free myths

10. MYTH: "Riding the buses and trains isn't safe."
TRUTH: Even the dumbest thugs know your RTA driver is a push-button call away from the RTA Police - one of the largest police forces in the state. And mile for mile, you're five times more likely to get into a traffic accident if you're driving a car than if you're riding transit.

9. MYTH: "It costs way too much to be without a car."
TRUTH: Trade in your car for a transit pass, a bicycle, and some comfortable walking shoes and your savings account will grow, not shrink, by thousands of dollars a year. In a few years, the savings will allow you to make the down payment on a nice home.

8. MYTH: "You can't bicycle year-round in Cleveland because of the weather."
TRUTH: Our summers aren't all that hot! (But seriously, winter weather can prevent bicycling at times. With proper clothing and equipment many Northeast Ohioans ride their bikes 10 months or more per year.)

7. MYTH: "Only poor people take buses and trains."
TRUTH: If you commute by car to downtown Cleveland, you're the one who will be feeling light in the wallet. A visual survey of all the business suits and briefcases on the buses and trains during rush hour will reveal that transit is for everybody.

6. MYTH: "Riding the bus isn't cool."
TRUTH: Saving money and the environment is always in style.

5. MYTH: "I'll lose my freedom if I don't own a car."
TRUTH: The design of most outer suburbs forces you to own a car. When you live in transit- and pedestrian-friendly neighborhoods, you have transportation choice and thus, more freedom.

4. MYTH: "You can't get a cab in Cleveland."
TRUTH: Downtown hotels and many neighborhood activity centers often have cabs waiting. And if you can't find a taxi in the Flats, you must have fallen in the river.

3. MYTH: "The only good place to walk in Cleveland is on a treadmill."
TRUTH: In many neighborhoods, you can do your errands and get your exercise in the same breath. A lot of people walk a lot farther in shopping mall parking lots than they would to get to the closest bus stop.

2. MYTH: "The city may offer more travel options, but the suburbs are quieter and less stressful."
TRUTH: You'll find that since many city neighborhoods have shopping and services close by, car traffic is low and so is the noise and stress.

1. MYTH: "In Cleveland, you just can't get where you're going without a car."
TRUTH: Read *Car-Free in Cleveland!*

Courtesy of Bradley Flamm

OTHER GREATER CLEVELAND TRANSIT AGENCIES

No other transit agency in Northeast Ohio comes close to the size or level of service of RTA. But there are nine other transit agencies that cover the rest of the region. They vary greatly, from Summit County's METRO system with over 30 regular bus routes to Geauga County's small Dial-a-Ride service for senior citizens and people with disabilities. Here's what you'll need to know to use them.

Car-Free in Cleveland

METRO Regional Transit Authority
Akron and Summit County

The METRO Regional Transit Authority is the second-largest transit agency in Northeast Ohio, offering over 30 regular bus routes and 11 special service routes throughout the city of Akron and the rest of Summit County. Regular service is available Monday through Friday, and additional service is available Saturdays on selected routes. There is no Sunday or holiday service.

The general one-way fare is $1.00, and the exact amount is required upon boarding the bus since drivers do not carry change. Students pay 65¢ and seniors (over 65 years of age) and people with disabilities pay 50¢. Up to two children can ride free with every fare-paying adult. Monthly passes and multiple ticket booklets are also available at discounted rates. Transfers between routes are free and good for one hour. Ask the driver for one when boarding the first bus of your trip.

METRO operates two "North Coast Express" direct bus routes between Akron and downtown Cleveland. One-way fare is $3.00. These buses operate on city streets in Summit County and then travel to and from Cuyahoga County on the interstates.

In addition, some METRO buses connect with RTA, such as METRO bus #101 with RTA bus #77F at the Veterans Administration Hospital in Brecksville. Check schedules for transfer times.

Please note that only those buses designated with a wheelchair symbol in the METRO bus route timetables are wheelchair accessible.

METRO CONTACT INFORMATION
☎ 330-762-0341 or toll-free at 1-800-227-9905
TDD: 330-996-7467
✉ 416 Kenmore Blvd., Akron, OH 44301
🖥 www.akronmetro.org

LAKETRAN
Lake County

LAKETRAN is the third-largest transit system in Northeast Ohio and serves Mentor, Painesville, Willoughby, Fairport Harbor, Madison and other Lake County destinations. Six fixed bus routes provide service within Lake County, Monday through Friday. Some buses also operate

Other Transit Agencies

on Saturdays, but the routes they service sometimes differ from weekday routes, so be sure to check a printed schedule or call the LAKETRAN Answer Line before setting your itinerary. There is no Sunday LAKETRAN service.

Bus stops along LAKETRAN's six fixed routes are located at major destinations and intersections and are indicated by LAKETRAN bus stop signs. Transfers between routes are free and can be obtained from the drivers. The one-way fare on the local fixed routes is 75¢. Seniors, people with disabilities, Medicare cardholders and children (ages 2-12) pay just 35¢. Exact change is required.

Four commuter routes provide rush-hour service between Lake County and downtown Cleveland. Commuter buses depart from Mentor, Madison, Willowick and Wickliffe. Park-n-Ride lots are located at the Mentor Civic Center, the Madison Village Fire Station, and Lakeland Community College. Gateway Flyer buses depart from these sites. Call LAKETRAN for scheduling information.

Park-n-Ride service and Cleveland Flyer service are $2 each way, or you can purchase 11 rides in advance for $20. LAKETRAN routes also connect with several RTA routes, including #39X, #39F and #39BX at Shoregate shopping center in Willowick. Please check RTA and LAKETRAN schedules for details.

Dial-A-Ride is a door-to-door assisted transportation system for all Lake County residents, with a special emphasis on senior citizens and people with disabilities. Travel is limited to Monday through Saturday for Lake County destinations and for Cuyahoga County medical facilities in the University Circle area (check with LAKETRAN for details). Fares are $3 each way for non-resident adults, $1 each way for Lake County residents, senior citizens with a Golden Buckeye Card, people with disabilities and children (ages 2 - 12). Trips outside of Lake county are slightly more expensive. Reservations are necessary, and space is limited.

LAKETRAN CONTACT INFO
☎ 440-350-1000, 440-942-6332 or toll-free at 1-800-400-1300
TDD: 1-800-560-deaf
✉ P.O. Box 158 Grand River, OH 44045
555 Lakeshore Boulevard, Painesville, OH 44077
🖱 www.laketran.com

Car-Free in Cleveland

University Circle Bus Systems
Cleveland

If you lead or would like to lead a more car-free lifestyle and you live, work or study within the University Circle area on Cleveland's east side, you're in great shape thanks to the five free shuttle bus services run by University Circle, Inc. (UCI). UCI is a nonprofit development and service organization working to support and advance the cultural, educational, health care, religious and social service institutions that are the pride of Northeast Ohio. Case Western Reserve University, the Cleveland Museum of Art, Severance Hall (home of The Cleveland Orchestra), major hospitals and many, many other outstanding institutions are along UCI's shuttle routes.

University Circle is easily accessible from the RTA #6 and #9 buses (and many others) and the Red Line Rapid transit trains. Once you're in the circle, UCI's shuttle services give you lots of choices.

Circlelink bus shuttles provide access to major University Circle destinations every 15 minutes from 6:15 a.m. to 5:30 p.m., Monday through Saturday and noon to 5 p.m. on Sundays. Circlelink can also get you to the Mt. Sinai Medical Center from 6:15 a.m. to 9:30 a.m. and 2:30 p.m. to 5:30 p.m. every half hour on weekdays. Pick-ups are at Circlelink bus stops only (look for the signs along the side streets). All Circlelink buses are wheelchair accessible.

The University Hospitals of Cleveland Shuttle (UHC Shuttle) provides transportation between the bus stops of major University Circle parking areas and various hospital locations. The UHC Shuttle is available every 20 minutes every day, 24 hours a day. Some, but not all, buses are wheelchair accessible.

The Route C CWRU Commuter Route shuttle buses link CWRU campus buildings with commuter parking lots along Euclid Avenue. Service is available every 10-12 minutes from 7:30 a.m. to 8 p.m. weekdays, but not during the summer and on major holidays. Some, but not all, buses are wheelchair accessible.

The three Campus Loop shuttle buses (the North Loop, the Campus Flyer and the South Loop) run continuously in the evenings from 6 p.m. to 12:45 a.m. every day. The North and South Loop buses arrive at designated stops every 12 minutes. The campus flyer arrives at designated stops every 10 minutes. Service for all routes

Other Transit Agencies

is reduced during school breaks, holidays and during the summer, and there is no service on Christmas and New Year's Day. Some, but not all, buses are wheelchair accessible.

> **UNIVERSITY CIRCLE CONTACT INFORMATION**
>
> All calls should be made between 8:30 a.m. to 5p.m.
> ☎ 216-791-6226 (CWRU students & employees use Extension 3228 or 3229)
> ✉ 12100 Euclid Avenue, Cleveland, OH 44106
> 🖥 www.universitycircle.org

Lorain County Transit

Lorain County Transit (LCT) provides fixed-route and Dial-A-Ride transit thoughout Lorain County with connecting service to the Greater Cleveland RTA system in Avon Lake and North Olmsted. LCT's fixed-route service includes five regular local bus routes that serve Lorain, Elyria, Oberlin, Avon, Avon Lake, North Ridgeville, Amherst, Wellington, LaGrange, Grafton and Sheffield Lake. Lorain County Transit bus signs are placed along the fixed route, but be aware that there are no fixed bus stops. To catch a bus simply wave to the driver anywhere along the route, on the same side of the street as the bus.

All fixed-route services are available Monday through Friday (except holidays), with most routes beginning service before 7 a.m. and ending by 6 p.m. Only the Lorain-Elyria-Oberlin bus provides weekend service. Please check individual schedules for times. Bus fares are $1.25 and should be paid in exact change upon boarding the bus (60¢ for senior citizens, people with disabilities and children ages 3 to 12; children under 3 ride free with paying adult). Monthly commuter passes are also available. Call LCT for prices and sale locations.

Commuter connecting service permits LCT riders to travel to Cuyahoga County destinations by connecting with the Greater Cleveland RTA Express Bus #31X in Avon Lake and RTA routes #75X and #63F in North Olmsted.

Dial-A-Ride and Need-A-Lift service is curb-to-curb service that is

Car-Free in Cleveland

available to Lorain County residents who live outside the fixed-route system. These services are provided by Avon Lake Dial-A-Bus, Oberlin Rural Transit Program and Vermilion Community Services in conjunction with Lorain County Transit. Days and hours of service are limited. Call the contact telephone numbers for details.

> **LORAIN COUNTY TRANSIT CONTACT INFORMATION**
> ☎ 440-949-2525 or 800-225-7703
> ☎ Avon Lake Dial-a-Bus: 440-930-4126
> ☎ Oberlin Rural Transit: 440-949-2525 or 800-225-7703
> ☎ Vermillion Community Services: 440-967-3314
> ✉ One Park Landing, 6100 S. Broadway, Suite 3100
> Lorain, OH 44053
> 🖱 www.loraincounty.com/lct.htm

Brunswick Transit Alternative

Brunswick Transit Alternative (BTA) is a transit agency that, not suprisingly, serves the City of Brunswick, in northern Medina County. Bus routes are operated by the BTA Monday through Friday from 6:20 a.m. to 6:20 p.m. during school months and 7:20 a.m. to 7:20 p.m. during the rest of the year. Saturday service is available from 10:20 a.m. to 4:20 p.m. No Sunday or holiday service is available.

Routes are identified on posted signs as either north (red N inside a square) or south (green S inside a triangle), but buses can be boarded anywhere along the route simply by hailing the driver. Fares are 25¢ for adults and students and 10¢ for seniors and people with disabilities (exact fare is required).

Transfers between routes are free. All buses are equipped with wheelchair lifts. Brunswick bus routes easily connect with the RTA system through morning and afternoon rush-hour bus service on RTA bus #451 along Pearl Road (US Route 42). Check BTA and RTA system schedules for details. Schedules may also be picked up at Brunswick City Hall and local libraries.

> **BRUNSWICK TRANSIT ALTERNATIVE CONTACT INFORMATION**
> ☎ 330-273-5855
> ✉ 4095 Center Road, Brunswick, OH 44212
> 🖱 www.brunswick.oh.us/BTA.htm

Other Transit Agencies

Kent State University Campus Bus Service
Portage County

The Kent State University (KSU) Campus Bus Service provides transportation for the public to and from Kent State University campus destinations and surrounding areas within Portage County. Service follows the academic calendar, so there are often fewer buses or no service at all during weekends, summer months and holiday breaks. Service on some routes begins as early as 6:30 a.m. and runs as late as 10 p.m. Call for detailed information.

KSU Campus Bus Service is free between bus stops within and adjacent to the boundaries of Kent State University. KSU students also ride free beyond the KSU service area if they show their student ID card. Fares for the general public are $1 (50¢ for people with disabilities and senior citizens) and should be paid on the bus with exact change or by using passes or tickets purchased in advance. Tickets and monthly passes are available by mail and at several sites in Ravenna, on the KSU campus and in Kent (call for specific sales locations).

There is also direct service to Akron ($2 each way or books of ten tickets for $16) and Cleveland ($5 each way, $7 round-trip or books of 5, 10 or more for $3.50 per ticket) that connects with RTA and METRO transit services. Other transportation services are available to help match riders to car pools and ride share opportunities. Some, but not all, buses can accommodate wheelchairs, and some buses are equipped with bike racks.

KSU CAMPUS BUS SERVICE CONTACT INFORMATION
☎ 330-672-RIDE
✉ 1950 State Route 59, Kent, OH 44240
🖰 www.kent.edu/ksuts/cbs

Portage Area Regional Transit Authority
PARTA

Outside of the City of Kent, where the Kent State University Campus Bus Service provides frequent transit service for car-free residents, Portage County is not a particularly good place to lead a car-free lifestyle. However, the Portage Area Regional Transit Authority (PARTA) does offer limited service with two scheduled fixed bus routes and Dial-A-Ride services

23

within the county for county residents.

The first fixed route provides service Monday through Friday (except holidays), 7 a.m. to 6 p.m., to Windham, Garrettsville, Freedom Township and Ravenna, with morning and afternoon trips available between Mantua and Ravenna. The second route is the Southeast Kent Circulator, offering service within the southeast portion of Kent. This route is available Monday through Friday (except holidays), 9 a.m. to 2 p.m. The service is flexible and drivers will travel up to 3/4 of a mile off route when requested in advance.

Dial-A-Ride service offers door-to-door service for Portage County residents. Reservations are required at least one day in advance, and round-trip reservations should be made at that time, if needed. Dial-A-Ride service is available Monday through Friday, 7 a.m. to 5 p.m. Drivers will pick you up at any address in Kent, Ravenna, Brady Lake, Franklin Township or Ravenna Township and take you anywhere within the PARTA service area. Service to other areas of the county is also available on a limited basis. All PARTA buses are wheelchair accessible.

PARTA CONTACT INFORMATION
☎ 330-678-1BUS or Toll-Free 800-673-1BUS
✉ P.O. Box 190, Kent, OH 44240

Geauga County Transit

Geauga County is another part of Northeast Ohio where living car-free is not very convenient, unless you live in one of the older towns' neighborhoods and you can walk or bike to work, school, shopping and other services. Geauga County Transit does provide service to county residents with a door-to-door transportation system geared towards the elderly and people with disabilities. Service is available Monday through Friday from 5:30 a.m. to 9 p.m. No fixed-route bus service is currently available. Reservations are required at least two days in advance, but no more than three weeks in advance. Same-day service is available, but riders must be flexible about their pickup time. All buses are wheelchair accessible.

Fares for destinations anywhere within Geauga County are $4 each way. Seniors, people with disabilities, and children ages 6 to 17 ride for $2. Children under 6 years of age ride free when accompanied by a paying adult.

GEAUGA COUNTY TRANSIT CONTACT INFORMATION
☎ 888-287-7190 or TTY 800-275-5777
✉ 12555 Merritt Road, Chardon, OH 44024

Medina County Transit

Medina County is still another part of Northeast Ohio where living car-free is difficult, unless you live in Brunswick (where Brunswick Transit Alternative provides service Monday through Saturday) or in downtown neighborhoods of Medina, Wadsworth and other older towns where walking and bicycling are convenient options.

Limited transit service is provided, however, by Medina County Transit with door-to-door service between any two locations within the county for county residents. There is also limited service available between Medina County destinations and several Summit and Cuyahoga County locations. Service is available Monday through Friday between 6 a.m. and 6 p.m., with evening and weekend service available by special arrangement.

Medina County Transit service also provides specialized services for older adults and persons with disabilities. Reservations are taken by phone between 8 a.m. and 3 p.m. up to two weeks in advance, but at least one day in advance. Capacity is limited.

One-way fares vary, based on distance traveled. The base fare for seniors and the disabled is $1.38 and goes up in 8¢ increments. Older adult passengers may ride without paying a fare, but are requested to make a donation. The full-price fare for the general public starts at $2.75 and goes up in 15¢ increments. Children under 6 ride free with an adult, as do people accompanying passengers with disabilities as personal aides.

Car-Free in Cleveland

Fare assistance is available to people with disabilities and for J.O.B.S. Program participants through the Medina County Department of Human Services. Call 330-225-7755 for more information.

MEDINA COUNTY TRANSIT CONTACT INFORMATION

☎ 330-723-3641 or TDD 800-750-0750
☎ Brunswick: 330-225-7100
☎ Wadsworth: 330-336-6657
✉ 3334 Meyers Road, Medina, OH 44256
🖱 www.co.medina.oh.us/transit/transit.htm

BICYCLES

The environment for bicycling in the Cleveland area has improved a great deal in recent years, thanks to the construction of new bike paths, with more on the way. While the overall climate for pedal-powered transportation is still less than fully supportive, don't rule biking out! It is absolutely possible, and often convenient, to meet many of your daily needs by bicycle in Greater Cleveland.

There are many reasons to give it a try. Bicycling-as-transportation is cheap, improves your health and reveals the sights, sounds and faces of neighborhoods. Plus, you'll never have to pay for parking.

For trips of a few miles or less, a bicycle trip can also be faster than waiting for the next bus or train, or even faster than driving yourself. On a bike, you're also "doing the right thing." You are not creating tailpipe fumes for others to breathe and you are making your community more livable, attractive and interesting. Most of all, practical urban bicycling can be fun, combining feelings of freedom and control with a sense of community connectedness that cannot be matched in a car.

Basic cycling needs

Just a few items are needed for successful urban bicycling. First, of course, you'll want a sturdy bike. It doesn't have to be expensive or flashy. In fact, it's better if it's not since you don't want to have your wheels stolen because they're so valuable. Then buy a good lock and a helmet. A mirror is optional, but quite useful, so you might try experimenting with one. A bell or horn is recommended, but a willingness to speak up or shout when needed can do in a pinch. Reflective gear and lights are indispensible if you're going to be riding after dusk. A bag and/or rear rack is helpful for trips to the store, library, etc. If you're new to the area, a detailed street map is a good idea, too.

You should also note that some communities (like Lakewood and Shaker Heights) require cyclists to wear helmets when riding their bicycles. Required by law or not, wearing a helmet just makes good sense.

Theft prevention involves using good locking techniques (such as a chain or u-lock placed through both the wheels and the frame), and choosing visible lock-up locations. You should probably also take detachable items (like lights) with you.

Neighborhood errands

Bicycles are ideal for those within-the-neighborhood trips: light shopping, going to the library, visiting friends and attending meetings. The City of Cleveland and its surrounding older suburbs are the best places for practical urban cycling. They have many low-traffic neighborhood streets which are parallel to the main roads and have a good mix of destinations (homes, offices, grocery stores and restaurants), so practical bicycling can be a convenient, positive experience.

Some of the better-known Cleveland neighborhoods that are truly bicycle friendly include Ohio City, Shaker Square, Tremont, Rockefeller Park/East Blvd., and to a lesser extent, Detroit-Shoreway and University Circle. Older suburbs that offer a bicycle-friendly experience include Cleveland Heights and Lakewood, as well as Shaker Heights, Brooklyn Center and Rocky River.

Newer suburbs often have subdivision-style streets (that is, lots of cul-de-sacs and few through-streets), so reaching destinations is a chore for all but the motoring public. These suburbs also have high-speed, high-traffic arterial streets that are distinctly bike-unfriendly, with destinations that are far apart. As a result, bicycling in a modern, suburban setting is often impractical and not very enjoyable.

Whether you live in a community that already is conducive to bicycling or not, there's always more that our local governments can do to improve conditions. Get involved in your community's plans to design streets that work not just for cars, but for bicycles and pedestrians, too. Help develop share-the-road programs, convenient and safe bicycle racks and dedicated bike lanes where needed.

You can get involved with the bicycle planning committee at the Northeast Ohio Areawide Coordinating Agency (NOACA), the Greater Cleveland transportation planning organization. The members of the committee are promoting a Bike City USA program to encourage and educate city officials about the things they can do to improve cycling conditions in their communities. Call Sally Hanley at NOACA for more information (216-241-2414).

"Bikes as Vehicles"

"Vehicle for a Small Planet"

"The automobile – which has brought industrial society a degree of individual mobility and convenience not known before – has long been considered the vehicle of the future. But countries that have become dependent on the car are paying a terrible price: each year brings a heavier toll from road accidents, air pollution, urban congestion, and oil bills. Today people who choose to drive rather than walk or cycle a short distance do so not merely for convenience, but also to insulate themselves from the harshness of a street ruled by the motor vehicle. The broadening of transport options beyond those that require an engine can help restore the environment and human health- indeed, the very quality of urban life."
– Marcia D. Lowe
The Bicycle: Vehicle for a Small Planet

Car-Free in Cleveland

Bike-friendly streets on your morning commute

Whether as regular commuters, or just occasional seekers of excitement and exercise, many people use bicycles to get downtown. None of the available routes are particularly beautiful or restful (at least as of this writing), but here are several possibilities for making your own two-wheeled trek to the city center.

Coming from the east: use Euclid Ave., Chester Ave., Wade Park to Payne Ave. or the Lakefront Bikeway (the bikeway shares a public road for a distance, but it's still a good route from the East Side to downtown).

From the west: try Lake Rd., Clifton Blvd., Franklin Blvd., or Detroit Ave.

From the south: Broadview, State, and Ridge roads all feed into Pearl Road, which eventually becomes West 25th Street as it approaches downtown. From West 25th, you can get on Scranton Rd., which will lead you into the Flats where you can cross the Cuyahoga River and ride into downtown.

If you're coming from the north: you'll probably want to use a canoe instead of a bike!

> **BY THE WAY**
>
> While there could always be more bicycle-friendly routes, try the east-west Chester Avenue or the new Lakefront Bikeway into downtown Cleveland, the north-south Belvoir Boulevard in the eastern suburbs, or the north-south Wooster Road in the western suburbs.

As you might imagine, these roads are busiest during rush hours and special events (particularly Indians and Browns games). If you can arrange your schedule to avoid peak times, your ride will be much improved. Even 15-30 minutes can make a big difference.

There are also several north-south bike-friendly streets away from the city center. On the West Side, look for West Boulevard and Wooster Road. On the East Side, try East Boulevard, Belvoir Boulevard or the Harrison Dillard bikeway along Martin Luther King Jr.

Plans are being made to extend the Lakefront Bikeway west of downtown and to extend the Ohio & Erie Canal Corridor's

Towpath Trail northward all the way to the Lakefront Bikeway (connecting in the Flats) from its current terminus at Harvard Road. When completed, these projects will vastly improve the everyday experience of cycling to downtown Cleveland.

For more information about the west extension of the Lakefront Bikeway, contact the Cleveland Planning Commission at 216-664-2210. For information on the planned Towpath Trail extension to the Lakefront Bikeway, contact the Cuyahoga County Planning Commission at 216-443-3700.

Terrain and weather

Terrain for cyclists in Cuyahoga County is generally not a challenge. The land west of the Cuyahoga River – and all lakefront routes – are fairly flat. The eastern half of the county is, geologically speaking, the western edge of the Allegheny Plateau and has hills that range from mild to steep, though the hills are never longer than a few hundred yards. Just gear down and take your time.

As for the weather, OK let's face it, Cleveland weather can occasionally be daunting if you're on a bicycle. But those who say bicycling in Cleveland is only doable six months out of the year are exaggerating. (Madison, Wisconsin is one of the most bike-friendly cities in the U.S. and its weather makes ours look almost tropical!) Sure you've got to dress warmly during some months, and rain gear isn't a bad idea either. Bicycling can still be a practical, enjoyable choice for most of the year if you're well prepared.

Winds in Northeast Ohio can be strong, but only occasionally present a significant challenge to the practical bicyclist. The breeze is usually from the west, though warm spring days are often brought by strong winds from the south, while blustery north winds from over Lake Erie occasionally buffet downtown.

Snowfall has been erratic in recent years, ranging from as little as 31 inches in a season (1997-98) to 102 inches (1995-96). For those inclined to consider winter riding, we note that snow doesn't always accumulate (especially on the West Side, which gets less snow than on the East Side), and street cleaning on main surface streets is usually excellent. With appropriate clothing and common sense visibility precautions, year-round cycling is feasible.

Car-Free in Cleveland

Ten Speed Gripes

Bicycle activists all have stories. Being verbally assaulted by motorists. Sideswiped by cars. Mangled by chuckholes. Fumigated by diesel exhaust. Slashed by broken glass. They think of themselves as urban deer, or stealthy alley cats down to their last lives.

With the hints in *Car-Free in Cleveland*, you know that things don't always have to be that rough. But cycling conditions could and should be a lot better, and some of the most commonly-heard complaints are well-founded.

The first complaint is that motorists just don't get it – can't understand that bicyclists have an equal right to the road. Drivers become outraged when they have to slow down behind a bike, as if the bicyclist is acting recklessly just by being in the street.

Second, transportation planners don't view bikes as a serious mode of transport. Bike facilities always seem to be "extras" tacked on to transportation plans if there is money left over from highway work. ⇩

Bicycles and public transportation

If you ride RTA's Rapid, you can usually find a safe bicycle rack at or near your station. But surprisingly, in light of progress being made in transit systems throughout the U.S., customers with bicycles are not yet accommodated on the buses and trains of the region's largest transit system, the Greater Cleveland RTA. Some smaller systems, such as the Kent State Campus Bus Service, however, welcome bikes on their buses. (Note that folding bicycles in a bag may possibly be brought onto all forms of public transportation without hassles, including RTA's buses and Rapid trains.)

Periodically, there have been calls for better RTA transit facilities and policies for bicycles. RTA planners are considering new bikes-on-transit policies and we hope they'll move ahead with them soon.

Your involvement in Alt-Trans Cleveland can make a difference in gaining full public transit access for the bicycling public (see the membership page at the back of this book). Additionally, you can call George Dixon, RTA Board President, or Joe Calabrese, RTA General Manager, at 216-566-5100 to voice your support for transit-bicycle integration in Greater Cleveland.

Intercity connections are a better story. Both Greyhound and Amtrak will accept a boxed bicycle as one piece of checked luggage at no extra charge. And airlines will accept boxed bicycles for a fee (often $50 each way).

Safety notes

This is what your mom would say if she were a cyclist: "Wear a helmet. Ride safely and defensively. Buy a bell to warn pedestrians of your approach. Lock up your bike when you go into a building. Always use lights and reflective gear when it gets dark. Familiarize yourself with the rules of the road (including appropriate hand signals). And be aware of other practical precautions for urban bicycling." (Oh, and one more thing: contact the Ohio Department of Transportation or your local City Hall for more information on bicycle laws and courses on safe cycling.)

Remember that in the colder months, darkness arrives before 6 p.m. Use proper equipment for night time visibility; this is Ohio law, and also essential for your own safety. Ask at bicycle shops for information and advice on helmet fit, mirrors, lights, reflective gear, and all other aspects of cycling safety. With a little knowledge, practical urban cycling can always be a fun and safe experience.

Recreational bicycling options

If you're looking for exercise and fresh air, you should know that our region has an excellent network of recreational multi-use paths. Unfortunately, only the newly opened Cleveland Lakefront Bikeway is easily accessible from downtown and nearby neighborhoods. It stretches east from North Coast Harbor and East 9th Street in downtown Cleveland to Lake Shore Boulevard in Euclid.

Halfway between downtown Cleveland

Ten Speed Gripes

Third, existing bike routes don't go places you need to go. Recreational paths through the Metroparks are nice, but most aren't functional transportation routes.

Fourth, bikes aren't linked to public transportation. In other cities, people can take their bikes on trains or load them on bus racks. But not here. You can bring all kinds of luggage and baby strollers on the Rapid, but not a bike.

Bike facilities for whom?

Another complaint is that even members of the local bicycling community do not all appreciate the transportation potential of the bicycle. The community is divided among high-tech racers, long-distance touring cyclists, rugged mountain bikers, utilitarian commuters, fitness buffs, and casual, weekend riders (the most common type). These groups all have different interests and needs. There's no common agenda, no unified voice.

See box on next page

Car-Free in Cleveland

Ten Speed Gripes

What they want

Some activists don't want special paths or lanes. They want wider curb lanes that can be shared by bikes and cars. Then both can operate equally as vehicles, but with more room to maneuver.

Many cyclists feel more secure in their own lane, and there will always be a need for a variety of bike facilities for people of different abilities and ages. But the overall goal is making streets less hostile for everyone - speed limits reduced to 20 mph so cars and bikes can mix more evenly, education of motorists to make them more tolerant, signage to warn car drivers of bicyclists, more promotion of bicycling so more drivers would be more aware of what it feels like to ride a bike in traffic, a bottle deposit law to reduce broken glass.

Serious cyclists also want bicycle parking in downtown garages and showers in the ⇩

---

and Euclid is Gordon Park, and here the Lakefront Bikeway connects with the recently-opened Harrison Dillard Bikeway along Martin Luther King Jr. Drive. This new link in the city's bikeway system connects the lakeshore route with the cultural attractions of University Circle.

A little farther out in Cuyahoga County, there are several good bikeway systems. The largest is that of the Cleveland Metroparks which has more than 100 bike-friendly miles of all-purpose trails in its "Emerald Necklace" of parks and reservations. Maps are available by calling the Metroparks at 216-351-6300.

On the east side of Cuyahoga County, look for friendly recreational cycling on North Park and South Park boulevards in Shaker Heights, the Bedford-South Chagrin Parkway, Fairmount Boulevard east of I-271, and Chagrin River Road.

To the south, check out the excellent Towpath Trail of the Cuyahoga Valley National Recreation Area, the new Metroparks Canal Reservation, and the North Royalton-Brecksville Metroparks Parkway.

On the west side of the county, look for the Cleveland Metroparks' Big Creek Parkway and Valley Parkway.

The cities of Mentor in Lake County and Avon in Lorain County are developing bike route systems that will be quite comprehensive when completed. Some of the other county metroparks districts are also building bike routes aimed at the recreational cyclist. Contact the NOACA bicycle committee (see below) for more information on obtaining maps of bike routes, lanes, and paths in

Bicycles

Cuyahoga, Lake, Geauga, Medina and Lorain Counties.

For the most part, all-purpose trails and bike paths are located away from commercial areas, so there is very little shopping or other services along the way. One exception is the Big Creek Parkway, which closely parallels the Pearl Road commercial district through Parma Heights and Middleburg Heights. Valley Parkway in the Rocky River Reservation is downhill from several shopping districts, including Kamm's Plaza/Lorain Road and downtown Berea. Otherwise, be sure to take along water, snacks and tube repair kits when you plan on taking a long ride.

Rental bicycles

No bicycle rental facilities with public transit access exist in Greater Cleveland yet to our knowledge. Alt-Trans Cleveland hopes that this problem can be remedied in the near future. Call your local bicycle shops for more information.

Community bicycling information

🚲 Cleveland Area Bicycling Association (CABA), P.O. Box 94226, Cleveland, OH 44101. Telephone: 216-522-2944.

🚲 *Crankmail* is a monthly newsletter that contains listings for the region's many local bicycle clubs and a monthly calendar of events. You can contact Crankmail at P.O. Box 33249, Cleveland, OH 44133-0249, by telephone at 440-877-0373, or on the Internet at www.crankmail.com.

Ten Speed Gripes

restrooms of work places. Employers should reward health- and environment-conscious employees who bike to work, instead of frowning because their hair is mussed from wearing a bike helmet.

But the bike activists know that none of this will happen without public support - much more support than we've seen to date. The disparate factions of the local bicycling community must come together around a common agenda and have a strong voice in regional transportation planning. They must involve neighborhood groups, clean air advocates and everybody else who will benefit from a more balanced transportation system and friendlier streets.

- Excerpted from "The Greater Cleveland Environment Book," by David Beach 🚲

Car-Free in Cleveland

🚲 Northeast Ohio Areawide Coordinating Agency's Bicycle Advisory Sub-Committee meets regularly to promote bicycling in all aspects of Northeast Ohio's transportation planning efforts. Contact Sally Hanley at NOACA, 1299 Superior Ave., Cleveland, OH 44114-3204. Telephone: 216-241-2414. Internet: www.noaca.org.

🚲 Ohio Bicycle Federation, 40 W. 4th St. #400, Dayton, OH 45402. Telephone: 937-463-2707 Internet: www.ohiobike.org.

🚲 *North Coast Sports* is a free monthly newspaper reporting on sporting events and sporting clubs throughout Northeast Ohio, including extensive coverage of bicycling. Pick-up a copy at many locations throughout the region (public libraries, bicycle shops, sports shops, and health clubs are good places to try) or contact North Coast Sports at 216-461-6630.

Courtesy of Greg Aliberti

MORE TRANSPORTATION CHOICES

Car-pooling, van-pooling

Do you live in a location that's not well served by transit, so you're stuck behind the wheel to get to work, day in and day out? Joining the commuter herd gets old fast. But there's a solution out there for Northeast Ohioans: RIDESHARE! is a free 14-county ride-matching service to help commuters establish car-pools.

RIDESHARE! is coordinated by Greater Cleveland's regional transportation and environmental planning agency, NOACA (the Northeast Ohio Areawide Coordinating Agency). NOACA maintains a list of motorists who are seeking partners to share their ride to

Car-Free in Cleveland

work. By sharing the driving and costs, car-poolers can save hundreds of dollars on gas, parking and other commuting expenses, as well as reduce highway congestion. They also have good company on the way to work.

NOACA coordinates a van-pooling program, too. Van-pools consist of seven to 15 commuters who share the cost of leasing and maintaining a van, plus parking and gasoline. One member of the group volunteers to drive the van and gets to ride free, while having unlimited use of the van on evenings and weekends. The Greater Cleveland area currently has seven van-pools operating.

One thing that discourages many people from considering car- or van-pool is the worry that they might get stuck at work without a car in an emergency. That's no problem with the RIDESHARE! program because commuters who participate in a car-pool or van-pool at least three times a week are eligible for the Guaranteed Ride Home program. The program covers 80 percent of the cost of a taxi ride home (up to a $60 maximum).

Contact NOACA to see if the car-pool or van-pool program meets your commuting needs. Or encourage your employer to call NOACA to arrange a presentation on car-pooling and van-pooling at your workplace.

> **NOACA CONTACT INFORMATION**
> ☎ 216-241-2414 or Rideshare Line 800-825-RIDE
> 📖 1299 Superior Ave., Cleveland, OH 44114-3204
> 🖥 www.noaca.org

Car rentals

Sometimes, despite all the car-free choices in Greater Cleveland, you need access to a car. Either you're going to places not well served by transit and too far away to bike, you're running a dozen errands to widespread locations, or you'll be coming home with lots of groceries and shopping treasures. If taking a taxi doesn't work well for you in those circumstances, you can always rent a car.

There are many car rental companies in the Greater Cleveland area, from the widely known national chains to small, locally owned companies with just a few cars. Car leasing and sales dealerships will also sometimes rent cars.

When renting a car, it's important to keep in mind a few questions about the rental company's policies.

More transportation choices

These include:

🚗 **How old do you have to be to rent a car?** Many car rental companies will rent to people 21 years old and up, but some require the driver to be 25 years old. Of course, you will be asked to show your driver's license when renting a car.

🚗 **What kind of insurance is required?** What kind of insurance can be purchased through the car rental agency? Inquire about collision and/or damage insurance provided by the car rental company. Sometimes it's included in your rental fee, and sometimes it's not. If you already have auto insurance, ask your insurance agent how much coverage you will have in the event of an accident while using a rented car. Remember that when you rent, you'll be driving an unfamiliar car and often in unfamiliar areas. Accidents do happen.

> **BY THE WAY**
>
> If you must drive to do some shopping at downtown's Tower City Center or for partying in the Flats, consider leaving your car at the city's Muny Parking lot (off the Shoreway) and take the Waterfront Line. Muny Parking is free on evenings and weekends, while a 4-hour pass for the Waterfront Line can be bought for $1.50 per person.

🚗 **Do you need a major credit card?** Many car rental companies require an imprint of a major credit card (MasterCard, VISA, American Express, Discover, etc.) to rent a car. Some may permit a cash deposit.

🚗 **How does the company charge renters for use of the car?** Agencies can offer unlimited mileage, flat fees, a charge per mile, by the day, the week, or a combination of these options.

🚗 **Are you expected to fill the gas tank before you return the car?** Agencies often charge high prices for gallons of gas that you use but do not replace – read the fine print!

Also, you should always check the condition of the car before you leave the agency's parking lot with a rental. You may be charged for existing scratches and dents if you do not mention them to the rental agent before you drive away.

The best listing of car rentals is in the phone book's Yellow Pages, under "Automobile – Rental and Leasing." The greatest concentration

Car-Free in Cleveland

of these agencies are located at Cleveland Hopkins International Airport, and you can get to them easily by taking RTA's Red Line train to the airport and then hopping into the car rental agency shuttle bus.

Agencies located downtown or in some of the centrally located neighborhoods and suburbs are also usually accessible by transit. If you decide to rent from a place that isn't easy to get to, ask if the car can be dropped off at your residence or place of work. But be aware that this might involve an extra fee.

Taxicabs

Need to get somewhere fast, at a late-night hour, from one area not well served by transit to another area not well served by transit, or with a group of people? Sometimes renting a car by the mile – that is, taking a taxicab – is your best choice. Cleveland isn't a taxicab city the way New York is, but there are several major taxicab services in the Greater Cleveland area, and arranging a ride is pretty straightforward.

All taxi companies charge a base fare, and then a set cost per 1/4 mile. Most taxi drivers lease their cars and are permitted to strike a deal for longer trips, off the meter. But you'll need to negotiate any off-the-meter trips with the driver, so you should only do so if you already have a good idea what the cost might be. Drivers of the larger mini-vans and full-sized vans also will deal with a full car of customers at one flat fee for short rides.

TAXI COMPANIES

Ace Taxi Service	216-361-4700
Akron Yellow Cab (Akron area)	330-253-3141
Americab	216-881-1111
Barberton Summit Taxi (northern Summit County)	330-825-9933
Falls Cab Company (Cuyahoga Falls)	330-929-3121
Maple Heights Cab Co. (southeast suburbs)	440-232-1222
North East Cab Co. (Willoughby)	440-953-0000
Ohio Cab Company (west side)	216-676-8889
Southwest Cabs (southwest suburbs)	440-237-3100
Westlake Cab Serv. (West Shore suburbs)	440-331-5000
Yellow-Zone Cab	216-623-1500

Taxis can be reserved by calling at the time you need transportation or up to a day or two ahead of time for specific trips (such as a ride to the airport). Call the dispatcher for details, and be sure to let them know if you need to be somewhere at a specific time (say, to catch a Greyhound bus). When you're on a set schedule, always give yourself plenty of time when calling for a taxi (at least couple of hours), especially if your trip does not originate from downtown Cleveland.

Taxis can also be flagged down on the street. But apart from downtown Cleveland, there are not a lot of empty cabs on the road, so don't rely on luck to find one when you need it. Look for recognized taxi stands at Hopkins Airport, in downtown Cleveland at all hotels, in the Flats, at the Rock and Roll Hall of Fame & Museum, and at Jacobs Fields/Gund Arena. Not all taxis are available 24 hours a day, so call for individual details. See the box on the previous page for a list of the major companies. Please note that some of the companies only provide service to limited areas of the region.

Water transport

Excellent water transportation is why Cleveland grew where it is. Commerce and industry demand speedy connections between the places where people make things and the places where people need them. In the nineteenth century, that meant water connections, and Moses Cleaveland (who founded the city in 1796) recognized the potential of this place situated along the shore of Lake Erie and at the mouth of the Cuyahoga River. The city grew slowly during the first few decades of its existence, but once the Ohio & Erie Canal was completed, linking the industry of Cleveland to the Ohio River and thus the Mississippi, things took off at a dizzying pace in the mid-1800's.

The canal's heyday only lasted a few decades, however. Once railroads were built and later when car and truck transportation became cheap and convenient, the need for transportation by river, lake and canal declined. Unless you were shipping iron ore, coal or steel, you could find simpler and more direct routes overland.

Today, Lake Erie and the Cuyahoga River are still served by commercial freighters, but water travel for most residents is strictly recreational. During the summer months, there are tourist and sightseeing trips of the lake and the river on the *Goodtime III* (located at North Coast Harbor next to the Rock & Roll Hall of Fame) and other commercial boats.

Car-Free in Cleveland

Also during the summer months, there is a convenient way of getting across the Cuyahoga River when you're in the Flats entertainment district. The Holy Moses Water Taxi ferries partiers and street roamers between the East and West Banks in the heart of the restaurant and bar district for $2 each way. The trip does not offer many thrills or chills, but it's an effective way to get from bar to bar without walking around to the nearest bridge at Center Street (but don't discount that option – it's a fascinating walk if you have the few minutes you need to make the trip on foot).

Walking

No, the title of this section isn't a joke. Walking is as much of a transportation option as buses, bikes and taxis. Certainly you're not going to travel from Cleveland Heights to Lakewood on foot. But if you're living and/or working in Cleveland Heights or Lakewood, walking can be an excellent way of getting yourself from point A to point B.

Of course, if you've read this far, you know that we'll tell you walking is good for you – you'll get a little exercise, that's for sure. We'll tell you it's good for the planet, too – you're not contributing to air, water or noise pollution when you're a pedestrian. And there's more to see and enjoy when you're on foot– you can't window-shop or stop to chat with a neighbor when you're speeding by in a car at 45 m.p.h.

Mostly, walking is just a good way to get around if you value the joy of *being* in a place more than the ability to *get away from it* as quickly as possible. Where streets are safe, speed limits are low, buildings come up to well-maintained sidewalks (instead of being hidden behind a sea of parking), where trees and greenery provide shade and scenery, where there is a good mix of residential and commercial uses, and pedestrians can see and be seen,

> **BY THE WAY**
>
> To avoid winter winds while walking in downtown Cleveland, try one of the many pedestrian passageways between buildings or under the wind-blown streets. Look for them around Tower City Center, in the arcades in the 500-block of Prospect, Euclid and Superior avenues, near the Convention Center, and under East 9th St.

More transportation choices

walking is simply one of the great pleasures of life.

Fortunately, it's easy to be a pedestrian in Northeast Ohio because Cleveland, Akron and their older suburbs are "pedestrian-friendly" in many places, especially in the downtown areas and town squares. You can bet that in a city or village with a long history, walking is a good transportation option. Having been built at a time when few people owned cars, they were designed to a human scale that makes walking convenient and enjoyable.

Weather is an issue when you're on foot, and you want to have the right clothing to make walking comfortable. Make sure you have an umbrella if it's raining, a warm jacket, gloves, and boots if it's cold, and maybe even a cool drink if it's hot.

In downtown Cleveland, there are even places where you don't have to brave the elements to get from place to place on foot. Many passages cut through building lobbies, walkways and parking structures where pedestrians can escape the cold, rain, snow, or just enjoy a change of scenery. Some of the most popular shortcuts include the Euclid Arcade, the Old Arcade, and the Colonial Arcade, all of which cut through the middle of city blocks and connect major thoroughfares.

Courtesy of Ken Prendergast

BEYOND CLEVELAND

Planning a weekend at Put-in-Bay? Visiting friends and family in Pennsylvania for the holidays? Traveling to Chicago for business? For the times you just need to get out of town, Greater Cleveland has a lot of great options for car-free residents. Whether you need to get to the airport, the bus terminal or the train station, expanding your horizons beyond Cleveland is easier than you think. Here are some ways to do it.

Greyhound Bus Lines

Greyhound services destinations throughout Ohio and North America, and also connects to airports and Amtrak train stations. Tickets for Greyhound bus service can be purchased at three Cleveland-area stations: Downtown (1465 Chester Avenue), in Maple Heights (20551 Southgate Park Boulevard) and in Parma (8003 Brookpark Road). Because lines can

Car-Free in Cleveland

sometimes be slow-moving, give yourself time if you're buying your ticket on the same day that you travel. Tickets can also be ordered by mail 10 days or more in advance by using a major credit card. Call 800-231-2222 for details. Greyhound offers discounts when tickets are purchased 30, 21, 14, or 7 days in advance. Discounts are also available for seniors, children, and military personnel.

Here are just a few of the cities that Greyhound serves from its downtown Cleveland terminal:

🚌 Akron: Ten trips a day in each direction, $6 one-way or $10 round-trip. Trips take between 45 minutes and 1 hour.

🚌 Columbus: Twelve trips a day in each direction for $16 one-way or $32 round-trip. Most trips take 2.5 to 3 hours, though some trips via Akron take nearly 5 hours.

🚌 Youngstown: Six trips a day in each direction for $12 one-way or $21 round trip. Trips take between 1 hour and 30 minutes and 2 hours.

🚌 Canton: Four trips a day in each direction, with more via connections at Akron. The fare is $14 one-way and $28 round trip. Travel time is 1.5 to 2 hours.

🚌 Mansfield: Four trips a day in each direction. Call 1-800-231-2222

BY THE WAY

There are lots of plans under way to make car-free living in Cleveland better. Here are the most important proposals:

• Extensions of the Red, Blue and the Green lines could increase access to existing employment, housing and shopping districts.

• Downtown Cleveland and Lorain transportation centers may be constructed, making it easy to transfer between buses, trains, and taxis.

• Commuter rail service is in the works that could speed riders west to Lorain, south to Akron and Canton, southwest to Medina, southeast to Solon and Aurora, and east to Mentor, Painesville, and Conneaut.

• Bike routes are planned along the entire Cleveland lakeshore, connecting the Flats to the Ohio & Erie Canal corridor.

• An extension of the Waterfront Line could create a downtown rail loop back to Tower City.

• RTA is planning new Community Circulator routes.

for fares. Direct trips take 1 hour and 40 minutes, with trips via Akron taking over 3 hours.

🚐 Pittsburgh, PA: Eleven trips a day in each direction, with more via connections at Akron. Fares start at $19 one-way and the trip takes 2.5 to 4 hours.

🚐 Detroit, MI: Six trips a day in each direction, with more via connections at Toledo. The fare is $21 one-way or $40 round trip with a travel time of 3 to 4 hours.

🚐 Chicago, IL: Six trips a day in each direction. One-way fare is $35 and round trip is $66. Travel time is 6 to 8 hours.

🚐 New York, NY: Three direct buses a day in each direction, with many more available via connections at Albany or Pittsburgh. The one-way fare is $76 and a round trip ticket is $145. Travel time is 9 to 15 hours.

Bus routes and schedules vary widely, and destinations are far more numerous than those shown above, so contact Greyhound for specific information. Their Web site at www.greyhound.com provides detailed scheduling information and fares.

Greyhound stations

Downtown: 1465 Chester Ave., Cleveland (216-781-0520). The downtown Greyhound terminal is within two blocks of RTA buses 1, 4, 6/6A, 7F, 8, 9X/BX/F, 14, all 15s, 19X, all 20s, 21X, 22, 23, 25B/W, 31X, all 32 express buses, 33, all 35s, 38, 46F, all 51s, as well as all 55s, 63F, 64F, 65F, 69, 75X/F, 76X/F, 77F, 81, 86F, 87F, 88X, 96F, 97X/F 246, 251, 326, and 451, plus LAKETRAN Cleveland routes and Akron METRO X60/X61 buses. Taxis are readily available.

East suburban: 20551 Southgate Park Blvd., Maple Heights, (216-663-1490). The Maple Heights Greyhound station is directly served by RTA 41A/C, 76X/F, 90X and 97F buses.

Amtrak

Amtrak, the nationwide passenger rail system, currently runs several daily trains to Cleveland and nearby Elyria including the "Pennsylvanian," which offers daytime trains to Chicago, Detroit, Toledo, Pittsburgh,

Car-Free in Cleveland

Philadelphia and many smaller towns. Another route serves downtown Akron's Amtrak station at Quaker Square.

You can make reservations by calling 1-800-USA-RAIL or by visiting Amtrak's Internet web site at www.Amtrak.com. Tickets can also be purchased on the train. Amtrak also provides single-ticket transfers to places not on rail lines via Amtrak motorcoach connections.

> **BY THE WAY**
>
> With the recent addition of long-distance daylight train service to Cleveland, Amtrak travelers can request that an RTA Waterfront Line Rapid stop to let them on or off at the Amtrak depot. Ask the RTA Rapid driver about it!

Here are a few cities which Amtrak serves from its downtown Cleveland station, 200 Cleveland Memorial Shoreway:

- Alliance/Canton: Two trains a day in each direction. One-way fares are $11-$20, and the trip takes slightly more than 1 hour.
- Boston: One direct train per day, with more via connections at Washington, D.C. and Philadelphia. The base fare is $63 one way; first-class accommodations cost more. Travel time is 15 hours.
- Chicago: Three trips a day in each direction. Fares are $45 to $82. Travel time is 6 to 7 hours.
- Detroit via a connection at Toledo: Three trips a day in each direction. Fares are $22 to $40. Travel time is less than 4 hours.
- New York City: One direct train per day, with more via connections at Pittsburgh and Philadelphia. One-way fares are $61 to $111; first-class accommodations cost more. Travel time is less than 12 hours.
- Pittsburgh: Two trips per day in each direction. One-way fares are $20 to $36. Travel time is about 3 hours.
- Sandusky: Two trains per day in each direction. One-way fares are $8-$15. Travel time is about 1 hour.
- Toledo: Three trips a day in each direction. Fares are $15 to $28. Travel time is 2 hours.
- Washington, D.C.: One direct train per day, with more connections via Pittsburgh and Philadelphia. Fares are $56 to $101. Travel time is about 9 hours.

Amtrak terminals

Downtown/Lakefront: 200 Cleveland Memorial Shoreway (216-696-5115 or 800-USA-RAIL). For transit access to the Amtrak Cleveland station take the RTA Waterfront Line Rapid (Blue/67X-Green/67AX lines). NOTE: you'll need to notify the Rapid driver that you are exiting at the Amtrak station as it is an "on-request" stop only. Also, RTA 39 and 247/Outer Loop buses, LAKETRAN Cleveland buses, and Akron METRO's X60 buses stop at East 9th St./North Coast, a 1/4-mile walk west of the Amtrak station.

Elyria: 410 East River Rd. at Bridge St., Elyria (800-USA-RAIL). For transit access to the Elyria Amtrak station, use Lorain County Transit's Elyria/N. Ridgeville route which connects to RTA 75X in North Olmsted and LCT's Oberlin buses.

Akron: 906 East Bowery St./Quaker Square, Akron (800-USA-RAIL). For transit access to the Akron station, use one of the many Akron METRO bus routes operating from the nearby Cascade Plaza. Call Akron METRO at 330-762-0341 or 800-227-9905 for details.

Airports

Cleveland Hopkins International Airport

Cleveland Hopkins International Airport is serviced primarily by Continental Airlines (Cleveland is a Continental hub), with additional service provided by Air Canada, American Airlines, America West Airlines, Comair, Delta Air Lines, Midwest Express Airlines, Northwest, Southwest, TWA, United Airlines, and USAir Express. Hopkins Airport services over 600 domestic and foreign departures and arrivals daily. Hopkins also offers a full range of airport services, including an airport hotel, retail plaza, restaurants, and both long- and short-term parking lots.

Cleveland is one of the few American cities with a rapid transit rail line which links its main airport terminal to downtown. The $1.50 Rapid ride on the Red Line (RTA 66X) between the airport and downtown takes about 25 minutes. Trains run every 12-30 minutes from 4:30 a.m. to 10 p.m. Between 10 p.m. and 12:40 a.m. a shuttle bus (RTA 66S) runs every 30 minutes to and from Public Square in downtown Cleveland. RTA 22 bus provides 1 a.m. to 3 a.m service from the airport to downtown via Rocky River Drive and Lorain Ave. Call RTA at 216-621-9500 for more information on the 66 S-route Rapid train/shuttle bus and the 22 route.

Car-Free in Cleveland

Taxis and several limousine services are available outside the baggage claim on the airport's lower level. For more information, call the airport at 216-265-6030. For specific details on flight destinations and schedules, call the individual airlines, or see a travel agent.

Akron/Canton Regional Airport

Located midway between its namesake cities, this growing airport provides service with major commercial airlines, including Airtrans, Comair, Continental, Northwest, United, US West, and USAir. For more information, call the airlines directly, or the airport at 330-896-2385.

See Destinations listings in this book on how to get from Cleveland to Downtown Akron (Cascade Plaza). Akron METRO RTA operates the X77 bus route from Cascade Plaza to the Akron/Canton Regional Airport. The buses run Monday-Friday (except major holidays), and travel time to the airport is 35 minutes. Departures from downtown Akron are at 6:20 a.m., 7:45 a.m., 11:20 a.m., 12:50 p.m., 3:20 p.m., and 4:50 p.m. Returning northbound, the X77 departs the airport at 7:00 a.m., 8:25 a.m., 12:05 p.m., 1:30 p.m., 4:05 p.m., and 5:30 p.m.

All Akron METRO buses connect at the airport with the Stark Area Regional Transit Authority's Route 115 buses to Canton and its northern suburbs.

Other airports

Other area airports offer freight and package service, small charter flights, as well as private airplane storage and services. These airports include: Burke Lakefront Airport, Lost Nation Airport, Cuyahoga County Airport, and Lorain County Airport. Call these airports directly for more information. (See the phone book's yellow pages under "Airports.")

> **BY THE WAY**
>
> There is 24-hour transit service available to Cleveland Hopkins International airport. While the Red Line Rapid serves Hopkins throughout the day and the Red Line shuttle bus runs until just after midnight, RTA's #22 bus to downtown Cleveland via Rocky River Drive and Lorain Road provides several middle-of-the-night trips to and from the airport.

Greater Cleveland major transportation terminals

Akron/Canton Regional Airport, Lauby Rd. and I-77, Green. ☎ 330-896-2385. 🚌 Directly served by Akron METRO X77 bus, which runs weekdays only from downtown Akron (Cascade Plaza). From Cleveland, take Akron METRO X61 (rush hours only) direct to downtown Akron. For more frequent service, take RTA 77F to the VA Medical Center and connect to Akron METRO 101 bus for Cascade Plaza.

Amtrak Lakefront Station, 200 Cleveland Memorial Shoreway, Cleveland. ☎ 216-696-5115. 🚌 Ride RTA Waterfront Line Rapid (Blue/67X-Green/67AX lines), and notify train driver that you are exiting at the Amtrak station walkway. Also, RTA 39 and 247 outer loop buses, LAKETRAN Cleveland buses, and Akron METRO's X60 buses stop at E. 9th St., at the top of the Shoreway's ramps, which is a 1/4-mile walk from the Amtrak station.

Burke Lakefront Airport, 1501 North Marginal Rd., Cleveland. ☎ 216-781-6411. 🚌 Ride RTA Waterfront Line Rapid (Blue/67X-Green/67AX lines), RTA 39 bus, LAKETRAN Cleveland buses, and Akron METRO X60 bus to North Coast Harbor Station, then walk over the Shoreway and turn east on North Marginal Road.

Greyhound-Downtown Station, 1465 Chester Ave., Cleveland. ☎ 216-781-0520. 🚌 The station is at E. 13th and Chester, which is within two blocks of RTA buses 1, 4, 6, 7F, 8, 9X/BX/F, 14, all 15s, 19X, all 20s, 21X, 22, 23, 25B/W, 31X, all express 32s, 33, all 35s, 38, 46F, all 51s, as well as all 55s, 63F, 64F, 65F, 69, 75X/F, 76X/F, 77F, 81, 86F, 87F, 88X, 90X, 96F, 97X/F 147 246, 251, 326, and 451, plus LAKETRAN Cleveland routes and Akron METRO X60/X61 buses.

Greyhound-East Suburban Station, 20551 Southgate Park Blvd., Maple Hts. ☎ 216-663-1490. 🚌 Directly served by RTA 41A/C, 76X/F, 90X and 97F buses.

Hopkins International Airport, 5300 Riverside Dr., Cleveland. ☎ 216-265-6030. 🚌 Directly served by RTA Red Line/66X/66S Airport station and RTA 22 bus (1 a.m. to 3 a.m.).

Car-Free in Cleveland

Greater Cleveland area cities and towns:

This section covers cities and towns in Northeast Ohio most of which are directly served from Cleveland by public transportation. Many of these cities are reached by connections with one or more public transportation systems. Places where connections can be made are noted here. For schedules, call the transit agency listed. Telephone numbers are listed at the front of this book.

AKRON - DOWNTOWN

Direct weekday service offered by Akron METRO bus X61 (rush hours only) or by daily Greyhound bus (to south side of downtown). On weekdays, you may also take RTA 77F bus to VA Medical Center and connect to Akron METRO 101 bus for Cascade Plaza. Or, on weekdays, take RTA 97F bus to Walton Hills Ford plant and connect to Akron METRO 102 bus for Cascade Plaza. Alternatively, on weekdays, take RTA 90X buses to Summit County Line and connect to Akron METRO 103 bus for Cascade Plaza.

AKRON - EAST SIDE

Direct daily service on weekdays is offered by Akron METRO X60 bus, or take RTA 97F bus to Walton Hills Ford plant and connect to Akron METRO 102 bus for Cascade Plaza.

AKRON - WEST SIDE

Direct service on weekdays is offered by Akron METRO bus X61 to Chapel Hill Mall, or, take RTA 77F bus to VA Medical Center and connect to Akron METRO 101 bus down West Market and West Exchange streets.

ALLIANCE

Direct service is offered by Amtrak or by Greyhound via a connection at Canton.

AVON LAKE

Direct service provided by RTA 31X bus.

BRUNSWICK

Direct service is offered by RTA 451 bus (rush hours only).

CANTON

Direct service is offered by Greyhound.

Beyond Cleveland

CHAGRIN FALLS
Direct service is offered by RTA 5 bus, which connects to RTA Blue Line/67X and other buses at Warrensville Center Road.

CHARDON
No regular route transit service is available to the county seat of Geauga County. You can try reserving a Geauga County Transit Dial-A-Ride bus from Chagrin Falls, which is the closest city to Chardon (served by RTA 5.)

CUYAHOGA FALLS
Direct service on weekdays is offered by Akron METRO X60 bus, or you can take RTA 97F bus to Walton Hills Ford plant and connect to certain Akron METRO 102 buses for Cuyahoga Falls Park-n-Ride. Also, on weekdays, take RTA 90X buses to Summit County Line and connect to Akron METRO 103 bus for eastern parts of the city along Howe Road.

ELYRIA
Direct service is provided by Amtrak and Greyhound. Or, on weekdays, take RTA 75X or 63F buses to the Lorain County line and connect to LCT Elyria/N. Ridgeville route for downtown Elyria, Midway Mall, and Lorain County Community College.

EAST LIVERPOOL
On weekdays, from September to May, take KSU's Campus Bus Service (for public and student use) from the Shaker Square Rapid station (RTA Blue/67X and Green/67AX lines) and University Circle Rapid station (RTA Red Line/66X) to the KSU Student Center and connect to Campus Bus Service's East Liverpool bus.

HIRAM
No regular transit service is available to this town, which is home to Hiram College. You can try reserving a Portage Area Regional Transportation Authority (PARTA) Dial-A-Ride bus from Solon, which is the closest city to Hiram that is served by RTA 41 bus.

HUDSON

On weekdays, take RTA 90X buses to the Summit County line and connect to Akron METRO 103 bus for central Hudson and industries along State Route 91.

KENT

On weekdays, from September to May, take KSU's Campus Bus Service (for public and student use) from the Shaker Square Rapid station (RTA Blue/67X and Green/67AX lines) and University Circle Rapid station (RTA Red Line/66X) to the KSU Student Center. On Saturdays, from September to May, a direct bus is offered from the KSU Student Center to and from Cleveland Public Square. On Fridays and Sundays, from September to May, Campus Bus Service serves alternating east side and west side Cleveland destinations.

LORAIN

On weekdays, take RTA 31X bus to Avon Lake and connect to LCT East Route bus for Meridian Plaza where other LCT bus connections can be made. Or, on weekdays, take RTA 75X or 63F bus to the Lorain County line and connect to LCT Elyria/N. Ridgeville route for downtown Elyria, Midway Mall, and Lorain County Community College.

MEDINA

No regular transit service is available to the county seat of Medina County. You can try reserving a Medina County Transit Dial-A-Ride bus from Strongsville or Brunswick, which is the closest city to Medina served by RTA (451, 51, or 89 buses).

MENTOR

Direct service is provided by LAKETRAN's 10 bus (rush hours only) from the Mentor Park-n-Ride. Or, on every day except Sunday, take RTA 39 bus to Shoregate Shopping Center and connect to LAKETRAN 3 bus. Also, on weekdays, take the RTA 49F bus to the Lake County line and connect to LAKETRAN 2 bus.

OBERLIN

Served daily by Lorain County Transit's Lorain-Elyria-Oberlin route. Connect to LCT Oberlin bus via Greyhound at Elyria Greyhound station. Or, take RTA 75X to LCT North Ridgeville bus, then connect in

Beyond Cleveland

Elyria to LCT Oberlin, or take RTA 31X to LCT East Loop bus, and connect at Lorain or Elyria to Oberlin bus.

PAINESVILLE

On Saturdays, take RTA 39 bus to Shoregate Shopping Center and connect to LAKETRAN 1 bus to Painesville. Or, on weekdays, take RTA 39 bus to Shoregate and connect to LAKETRAN 3 bus to Great Lakes Mall and connect to LAKETRAN 1 buses to Painesville.

RAVENNA

On weekdays, from September to May, take KSU's Campus Bus Service (for public and student use) from the Shaker Square Rapid station (RTA Blue/67X and Green/67AX lines) and University Circle Rapid station (RTA Red Line/66X) to the KSU Student Center, and connect to Campus Bus Service's Ravenna bus to downtown Ravenna and Robinson Memorial Hospital.

SANDUSKY

Direct service is offered by Amtrak and Greyhound.

TWINSBURG

Direct service offered by Akron METRO bus X61 (weekdays only) to Twinsburg's town center and nearby industries. Or, on weekdays, take RTA 93 and 97X buses to the Summit County line and connect to Akron METRO 103 bus.

WARREN

Direct daily service is provided by Greyhound. On weekdays, from September to May, take KSU's Campus Bus Service (for public and student use) from the Shaker Square Rapid station (RTA Blue/67X and Green/67AX lines) and University Circle Rapid station (RTA Red Line/66X) to the KSU Student Center and connect to Campus Bus Service's Trumbull Campus bus.

YOUNGSTOWN

Direct daily service is provided by Greyhound.

Places to see and things to do

Courtesy of Greg Aliberti

PLACES TO SEE & THINGS TO DO

Neighborhoods to visit - and to live in

Greater Cleveland is a region of great diversity. Not only is there a wide variety of ethnic groups, but the neighborhoods in which Greater Clevelanders live are just as diverse. You can find quiet, green suburbs, rocking city neighborhoods, communities in which to polka or jazz it up, or areas to commune with nature. Whether you've lived here all your life or you're visiting for the first time, there are a thousand places for you to explore and make new discoveries.

Fortunately, you can do all of these things car-free. This chapter describes Cuyahoga County neighborhoods and communities which are pedestrian-friendly, transit-friendly, or both. It focuses on neighborhoods that contain major tourist destinations, historic homes, or ethnic

Car-Free in Cleveland

Neighborhoods

What makes a place friendly to car-free folks?

- Compact neighborhoods with a good mix of different kinds of buildings, so that homes, apartments, stores and offices are close to each other, not miles and miles apart.
- A mix of housing types so that a diverse group of people can enjoy living in the same neighborhood – doctors and lawyers rubbing elbows with firemen, store clerks, teachers, students and retired folks, just like they have in small American towns for centuries.
- Good connections between streets, so that you can get to the places you're going easily and by a variety of routes. Suburban, cul-de-sac subdivisions often make children who live just a few hundreds yards apart walk a mile or more to see each other because access is thwarted by the design of the road network.
- Well-maintained sidewalks so that pedestrians don't have to leap over cracked pavement or dodge trash and dog poop.
- Uncongested and narrow streets where cars drive slowly, so that walkers and bicyclists feel safe.
- Streets that have been designed to a human scale, which very simply means that people feel comfortable and ⇩

enclaves, along with transit-friendly suburbs, and a few suburbs with major employment centers.

So forget about filling up on gas or feeding parking meters. And leave the worries about traffic jams to somebody else. Just pull out that transit pass, get your bike, or lace up those walking shoes and go explore!

CLEVELAND DOWNTOWN

Downtown Cleveland used to be a business district that was abandoned each day after 5 p.m. In recent years, however, it has become more of a 24-hour neighborhood with a growing supply of nightclubs, restaurants, shopping districts, and housing. The major hubs of downtown activity are Playhouse Square, the Gateway complex of Jacob's Field and Gund Arena, Tower City Center on Public Square (in the city's geographic and transit heart), the Warehouse District, and the Flats along the Cuyahoga River.

The revitalization shows in downtown Cleveland's residential population, which has grown by more than 100 percent since 1990 to exceed 10,000 residents. More housing is coming, especially along Euclid Avenue.

THE FLATS

On the banks of the lower Cuyahoga River, the Flats, Cleveland's party center. On a typical summer weekend night, thousands of revelers will drink, eat and dance in the Flats. If you like people watching, the Flats is the place to be. The Flats served by two Rapid stations: Settlers Landing, and Flats East Bank.

During the summer, to reach the West bank of the Flats, take the Holy Moses Water Taxi, which departs from near the Flats East Bank Rapid station. At all other times of the year, walk from the Settlers

Places to see and things to do

Landing Rapid station and cross the Cuyahoga River on the Center Street bridge.

The Flats and the nearby Warehouse District complement each other. The Flats has more dance nightclubs, which flourish mostly during milder weekend nights. The Warehouse District, by contrast, is primarily residential, with jazz and blues nightclubs that thrive even during the winter months.

THE WAREHOUSE DISTRICT

This downtown neighborhood (bounded by W. 3rd and W. 9th streets, Lakeside and Superior avenues) contains many warehouses and other structures built in the late 1800s and today house loft-style apartments, commercial offices, nightclubs, restaurants, and shops. The Warehouse District is on most bus routes going into the west side of Cleveland (including RTA 46F, 55, and 75X) plus some east side routes (RTA 1, 8, 14, 15, 19, 33 and 35 buses). It is also between the Tower City and West 3rd/Stadium Rapid stops (about a 5-minute walk from both stations). The eastern part of this area is served by a number of LAKETRAN and Akron METRO buses.

GATEWAY/LOWER EUCLID AVENUE

The area between Public Square and Playhouse Square and south of Euclid Avenue is rapidly being redeveloped with new housing, restaurants, shops and entertainment venues. About a dozen apartment buildings exist in this district, with more on the way. Nearly all RTA buses serve this district, and the Tower City Rapid station is at Public Square. This area is also served by a number of LAKETRAN and Akron METRO buses.

The district features several prominent attractions, including Jacobs Field (the home of the Cleveland Indians) and Gund Arena (the home of the Cleveland Cavaliers, Rockers

Neighborhoods

welcome on it: buildings are pulled up to the sidewalk (not separated from it by a small ocean of parking spaces) and they have windows so that pedestrians can see and be seen, trees and landscaping provide shade and greenery, and benches and trash bins let you take a rest and dispose of garbage.

• Frequent, high-quality, and inexpensive transit service so destinations outside of walking or biking distance are just an easy bus or Rapid ride away.

Some of the best Cleveland neighborhoods for going car-free are Chinatown, Detroit/Shoreway, Edgewater, Fairfax, Gateway/Lower Euclid, Little Italy, Ohio City, Shaker Square/ Larchmere, Slavic Village, Tremont, and the Warehouse District. Cleveland Heights, Euclid, and Lakewood are some of the best car-free suburbs in Northeast Ohio.

Unfortunately, far too many outlying suburbs don't offer land use patterns and transit services that permit low-mileage lifestyles.

However, some suburbs do have historic town centers that are pedestrian- and bicycle-friendly, with some transit service. These include Rocky River, Medina, Chagrin Falls, Painesville, Oberlin and Willoughby.

Car-Free in Cleveland

and Lumberjacks). For ticket information, call the Indians at 216-241-8888, the Cavaliers and Rockers at 216-420-2200, and the Lumberjacks at 216-420-0000. Gund Arena and Jacobs Field are linked to the Tower City rapid station by a covered walkway.

The Arcade, built in 1890, is one of America's oldest and most beautiful shopping malls. It has five stories of offices, eateries, and small shops, and contains grand marble stairways, gargoyles, and other elegant interior details. The Arcade is between E. 3rd and E. 6th Streets, and joins Euclid Avenue and Superior Avenue. The Arcade is also several blocks east of the Tower City Rapid station and bus hub.

The Euclid and Colonial Arcades, located between E. 4th and E. 8th streets, are turn-of-the-century shopping promenades, linking Euclid and Prospect avenues. These are being redeveloped with hotels, restaurants, and shops.

PLAYHOUSE SQUARE

The Playhouse Square complex (216-771-4444) is the third-largest performing arts district in the nation. It includes five major theaters hosting the Cleveland Opera, the Cleveland Ballet, the Great Lakes Theatre Festival, and a diverse schedule of theater and musical performances. The Playhouse Square box office is at 1519 Euclid Avenue. It is a short (2/3 mile) walk from the Tower City and North Coast Rapid stations, and is on the 6, 9, 35, 51, 55, 65, 69, 76F, 77F, 86F and 97F bus lines. Also, this area is directly served by all LAKETRAN and Akron METRO buses to Cleveland.

NORTH COAST HARBOR

This is Cleveland's newest tourist destination, with attractions such as the Rock and Roll Hall of Fame & Museum, the new Cleveland Browns Stadium, the Great Lakes Science Center, USS Cod submarine, and Steamship William G. Mather Museum. North Coast Harbor is just north of the Waterfront Line Rapid transit, between W. 3rd and E. 9th streets and North Marginal Road. It is served by the North Coast and W. 3rd Street rapid stations. Access by bus is via RTA's 39, 46, 55, 75, 79 and 81 buses. Also, this area is served by a number of LAKETRAN and Akron METRO buses and Kent State University's weekend Cleveland bus service.

The Rock and Roll Hall of Fame & Museum (216-781-7625) is a large museum devoted to, as you might guess, rock music and its history. For those without extensive record collections, the most interesting part of the Rock Hall might be the listening booths where you can hear the rock songs of the past. You can also hear older genres of music from which rock music evolved (such as country and rhythm/blues).

Places to see and things to do

The Great Lakes Science Center (216-694-2000) is a large, interactive museum with over 350 hands-on exhibits. The Science Center's OMNIMAX theater has a six-story high movie screen that gives guests an uncommonly realistic viewing experience.

PUBLIC SQUARE & TOWER CITY

Any visit to Cleveland should begin with its true center: Public Square and the neighboring Tower City Center complex. Tower City is a large shopping mall and transit hub developed from Cleveland's one-time railway station. All of Cleveland's Rapid lines, and most of its buses (RTA, LAKETRAN and Akron METRO), converge at Tower City.

At Tower City's doorstep is Public Square, a park that divides the city's east and west sides. Many American cities, even those which are more transit- and pedestrian-oriented than Cleveland, lack an identifiable center, but Cleveland's is undoubtedly Public Square. Public Square was laid out as a village green in 1796, when Moses Cleaveland (for whom the city is named) arrived to survey the land for New England investors. A statue of Cleaveland stands in Public Square's southwest corner. During the winter, a skating rink is established in the square's quadrant in front of Tower City. In Public Square's southeast quadrant stands the 127-foot high Soldiers and Sailors Monument, dedicated in 1894 to the more than 10,000 Cleveland-area Civil War soldiers and sailors. Public Square is surrounded by Tower City, numerous office buildings, and the Old Stone Church, built in 1853.

CLEVELAND NEIGHBORHOODS EAST OF DOWNTOWN

CENTRAL

The Central neighborhood today is the site of new housing development, much of it located in the Central Commons area. RTA's 8 (Cedar), 33 (Central), 35 (Quincy), 25 and 14 (Woodland/Kinsman) routes run east-west, with the 16 (E. 55th) running north-south. RTA's Rapid transit Red (66X), Blue (67X) and Green (67AX) lines run along the neighborhood's southern boundaries, with stations at E. 34th and E. 55th streets. *6-13 min. from downtown*

CHINATOWN

Many Asian-American businesses are concentrated northeast of downtown between E. 29th and E. 40th Streets, along Superior, St. Clair and Payne avenues. Asia Plaza is a miniature shopping mall at E. 30th Street and Payne Avenue. It includes an

Asian grocery store, a variety of other Asian-oriented businesses, and Li Wah, a restaurant known for its dim sum. Many other Asian restaurants and grocers exist in the neighborhood. Asia Plaza itself is on the 4 and 38 routes, and is a block from Superior Avenue (on the 326 route) and two blocks from St. Clair Avenue (on the 1 route). Other buses serving this area include the 6, 7F, 9, and 16A on Euclid Ave. The St. Clair Community Circulator/803 links all of the bus routes. *5-10 min. from downtown*

COLLINWOOD
Collinwood begins at around E. 140th Street, ends at the Euclid/Cleveland boundary at E. 185th, and runs along St. Clair and Lake Shore Boulevard. Collinwood is served by a variety of buses, including the 1, 30, 34, 37, and 39. *20-30 min. from downtown*

GLENVILLE
In Glenville, whose heart is at St. Clair Avenue (RTA 1) and East 105th Street (RTA 10 bus), dozens of new and rebuilt homes exist, with more on the way. Most of Glenville's homes were built in the late-1800s, with many of the new homes reflecting the historic architecture. The East Side Market, a bazaar of fresh food merchants, was built in the mid-1990s on the northeast corner of St. Clair and East 105th. It complements the Glenville Plaza. *20-30 min. from downtown*

HOUGH
Urban development first came to Hough during the Civil War. After extensive disinvestment and abandonment in the 1960s and '70s, Hough has now undergone an amazing renaissance. The neighborhood is primarily residential, with some corner store retail, and is very pedestrian-oriented. Major RTA east-west bus lines are the 38 (Hough) and 4 (Wade Park), with the north-south routes consisting of the 16 (E. 55th), 2 (E. 79th), and 10 (E. 105th). *8-14 min. from downtown*

FAIRFAX
Fairfax is home to some of the most exciting redevelopment efforts on the east side. Many of these developments are built with the pedestrian and transit user in mind and are located along busy bus and Rapid rail lines.

Hundreds of new and renovated homes are at Bicentennial Village, near E. 87th and Quincy Avenue, along with 70 new townhouses at Beacon Place, near E. 83rd, between Euclid and Chester avenues. Beacon Place is just east of Church Square, so-named because of the wide variety of historic houses of worship there. Church Square has new buildings and retail plazas.

Places to see and things to do

At the northeast corner of the Fairfax district, is the one of the city's largest employers the Cleveland Clinic Foundation. Fairfax also has two historic theaters: the Cleveland Play House and Karamu House. East-west RTA bus routes are the 8 (Cedar), 25 (Woodland), 35 (Quincy), 33 (Central), 32 (Carnegie), plus the 6, 7, and 9 (Euclid). North-south RTA buses are the 2 (E. 79) and the 10 (E. 105). RTA's Rapid transit Red Line (66X) runs through the neighborhood's southern boundaries, with stations at E. 79th and E. 105th-Quincy (both of these stations are likely to be relocated in a few years). *10-15 min. from downtown*

LITTLE ITALY

Cleveland's Little Italy (also known as Murray Hill) is a short walk or bicycle ride from the cultural attractions of University Circle. Most of Little Italy's restaurants and bakeries are along the main drag of Mayfield Road. Little Italy is also home to numerous studios and art galleries.

Little Italy is a few blocks south of the Red Line's (66X) Euclid-E. 120th Rapid station (which is slated to be moved to Mayfield Road in a few years). The neighborhood is also right on RTA's 9 bus route, and is served by University Circle Inc.'s CircleLink. *20-25 min. from downtown*

ST. CLAIR

The St. Clair community, located on St Clair Avenue between E. 55th and E. 70th Streets is easily accessible on RTA's 1 bus that goes up St. Clair Avenue. You can also take the Rapid to E. 55th and take RTA's 16 bus north from there. Other buses that serve parts of this area include the 2, 326 and 803/St. Clair Circulator buses. *15min. from downtown*

SHAKER SQUARE/LARCHMERE

Shaker Square is a tiny neighborhood that borders the suburb of Shaker Heights. Shaker Square, along with the nearby Larchmere district, is a compact area with Georgian-style architecture, with offices above many shops and restaurants. There are sidewalk cafes on the square, and apartment buildings, historic condominium towers and single-family homes just off the square. Shaker Square, like Shaker Heights, was designed by real estate developers Oris and Mantis Van Sweringen during the 1920s and is one of the nation's first planned, transit-oriented, mixed-use developments.

The Shaker Square and Larchmere shopping districts are served by the Shaker Square Rapid station of the Green (67AX) and Blue (67X) Lines. Just east of the square is the Drexmore stop (Blue Line) and Coventry stop (Green Line). RTA's 25, 48 and 50 buses also

Car-Free in Cleveland

serve this area. Finally, Kent State University's Campus Bus Service (330-672-RIDE) runs several buses a day each weekday from September to May between Shaker Square and Kent State University. *15 min. from downtown*

SLAVIC VILLAGE, PART OF THE SOUTH BROADWAY NEIGHBORHOOD

Built in the 1880s, Slavic Village is a great neighborhood in which to hop off the bus, take a stroll (especially along Fleet Avenue) and enjoy the sights of old-world cultures and the smells of ethnic cooking. Slavic Village boasts numerous bakeries, meat markets, and restaurants.

The commercial hub of Slavic Village (Broadway near Fleet Avenue) is served by the 19, 76X, 88X, 90X, and 97X buses (all of which run from downtown along Broadway, which intersects with Fleet Avenue). The RTA 16 runs south from the E. 55th Rapid Red line (66X) station. The fringes of this area are served by the RTA 10 and 15 buses.

To the south is the acclaimed Mill Creek housing development, located along Turney Road and RTA's 76X bus route, and part of the 10 route. Mill Creek consists of more than 200 new, traditionally designed homes, built in the 1990s around a town square and park. *15-20 min. from downtown*

UNIVERSITY CIRCLE

Most of Cleveland's premier cultural institutions are here, including its world-renowned symphony orchestra, its most prestigious museums, and Case Western Reserve University. In addition, University Circle is also the second-largest employment center in Greater Cleveland (trailing downtown) due to the presence of two large hospital and research centers (Cleveland Clinic Foundation and University Hospitals of Cleveland) and related institutions.

Most of University Circle's attractions are between Martin Luther King, Jr. Boulevard and Mayfield Avenue, and are either on Euclid Avenue (the area's main commercial street) or near East Boulevard north of Euclid. Do not attempt to see all of these attractions in a day; the Cleveland Museum of Art alone should take you several hours to tour.

The most noteworthy University Circle attractions are:
- The Cleveland Museum of Art, 1150 East Blvd., (216-421-7340).
- The Cleveland Museum of Natural History, 1 Wade Oval, (216-231-4600).

Places to see and things to do

- Severance Hall, home of Cleveland's symphony orchestra, 11001 Euclid Ave., (216-231-1111).
- Rainbow Children's Museum, 10730 Euclid Ave., (216-791-7114).
- The Western Reserve Historical Society and the Crawford Auto Aviation Museum, both located at 10825 East Blvd., (216-721-5722).

University Circle has three Rapid stops, all on the Red Line (RTA 66X). The University Circle Rapid station, the main transfer point for buses to most eastern suburbs, is near the corner of Cedar Avenue and Martin Luther King, Jr. Boulevard, several blocks south of Euclid Avenue. The Euclid/E. 120th stop is about 3/4 of a mile from most University Circle attractions, while the East 105th/Quincy stop is at University Circle's southwestern fringe. However, the Euclid/E. 120th station is slated to be relocated to a more convenient site in a few years.

RTA buses serving the area include the 6 (which run 24 hours a day), 4, 7, 8, 9, 10, 32, 38, 48, and 50. These run through University Circle or stop at the University Circle Rapid station. Also, Case Western Reserve and University Circle, Inc. (216-791-3900) run shuttle buses through the neighborhood. Finally, Kent State University's Campus Bus Service (330-672-RIDE) runs several buses each weekday, from September to May, between University Circle and Kent State University.

BY THE WAY

Three transit systems from areas outside Cuyahoga County serve Cleveland with regular bus service. Akron Metro Regional Transit Authority has two flyer bus routes for weekday commuters traveling to downtown Cleveland or Akron and northern Summit County. LAKETRAN has four weekday flyer bus routes from cities in Lake County for people working in downtown Cleveland, plus special trips to sporting events at Gateway. Kent State University's Campus Bus Service has several weekday buses from the Rapid stations at University Circle and Shaker Square to Kent (and surrounding cities), as well as limited service on weekends.

12-20 min. from downtown

CLEVELAND NEIGHBORHOODS WEST OF DOWNTOWN

DETROIT/SHOREWAY

West of Ohio City and east of the Edgewater neighborhoods is the Detroit/Shoreway district. This neighborhood features a good mix of housing, shops, and entertainment venues. The heart of the Detroit/Shoreway neighborhood is at W. 65th and Detroit Avenue. Here, you can find the Gordon Square Arcade (a 1920s-era shopping and apartment complex), funky nightclubs like the Brillo Pad, not to mention the alternative Cleveland Public Theatre. The district is being revived with new housing and rebuilt historic homes along Franklin Boulevard.

Walking and biking are pleasant, especially on Franklin Boulevard. And Detroit/Shoreway will soon be the site of Cleveland's first "ecovillage," an environmentally friendly neighborhood where traditional urban design and green building techniques create a garden neighborhood within the heart of the city. Transit services are extensive, with 24-hour service on the 326 and 22 bus lines. Other bus routes in the area include the 25, 45, 69 and 78. Two Red line (66X/66S) Rapid stations serve the area: W.65th-Madison station (RTA plans call for the renovation of this station in the coming years with access from Lorain Avenue) and the newly rebuilt West Boulevard station (formerly W.98th/Detroit).   *15-20 min. from downtown*

EDGEWATER

This Cleveland neighborhood lies along the Lake Erie shore, nestled between Edgewater Park and the Lakewood/Cleveland border at W. 117th Street. The major transit route is along Clifton Boulevard, and to a lesser-degree along Detroit Avenue. The neighborhood has some older mansions and 1920s-era apartment buildings north of Clifton, with mostly single-family homes, duplexes, brownstone apartment buildings and funky restaurants south of Clifton Boulevard.

Edgewater has excellent transit service. RTA's 45, 46F, and 55 buses all run up Clifton Boulevard towards Lakewood, while Edgewater's southern fringe is served by the 326, 25, 65X and 75X. The western border, at W. 117th, has the 50 bus, in addition to the Lakewood Community Circulator/804. Edgewater is served by two stations on the Red Line (66X/66S) Rapid. One is the West Boulevard (formerly W. 98th) station with the other being the W. 117th/Madison Rapid station.   *15 min. from downtown*

OHIO CITY

Ohio City is one of Cleveland's oldest neighborhoods, incorporated as a city in 1836 and annexed by Cleveland in 1854. Because of its age, the neighborhood is probably the city's most pedestrian- and bicycle-friendly. It has tree-shaded sidewalks, narrow streets and alleys, and historic homes–some within arm's reach of each other.

Ohio City's star attraction is the West Side Market at W. 25th Street and Lorain Avenue, next to the W. 25th Street Rapid station on the Red Line (66X) and is served by the 20, 21X, 22, 35 and 79 buses. The West Side Market is home to hundreds of vendors representing many ethnic groups. Ohio City also has numerous interesting shops and restaurants within a few blocks of the West Side Market. Other buses serving Ohio City include the 326, 25 and the Tremont Community Circulator/807, which operates on W. 25th Street before turning east to Tremont and south to Brooklyn Centre. *5 min. from downtown*

OLD BROOKLYN

This neighborhood near the city's south border has been made somewhat famous by the popularity of the Drew Carey show (Carey is an Old Brooklyn resident). Two revived commercial centers exist in Old Brooklyn: one at Pearl Road and Denison Avenue, the other at the confluence of Pearl, Broadview, Memphis, and State Roads. These commercial centers are within easy walking distance of Old Brooklyn's residential areas.

Most of Old Brooklyn is south of the Cleveland Metroparks Zoo, west of the Cuyahoga River and north of the city limits. There is excellent bus service to Old Brooklyn, including RTA's 20 (A, B, & X routes), 21X, 23, 35, 45, 51X, 68, 79, 50 and 98 buses. Also, the Tremont Community Circulator/807 links the W. 25th Street/Denison area to Ohio City and Tremont. *15-30 min. from downtown*

TREMONT

This is another pre-Civil War neighborhood, though some sections were built shortly before 1900. Tremont is immediately south of downtown and Ohio City. A section of Tremont, particularly along Professor Road, is like a self-contained small town, but with big-city art galleries and restaurants. Tremont is well known for its diversity. In fact, it is so diverse that one church, St. John Cantius, conducts services in English, Polish and Spanish.

In addition to its churches, Tremont has beautiful, old apartment buildings and condominiums such as Lemko Hall and the Lincoln Baths. Tremont's northern edge is about 1/2 mile from the Ohio City Rapid station, and the 81 bus goes through the heart of Tremont. The 23 bus serves W. 14th Street on Tremont's western fringe. RTA also offers the Tremont Circulator/807, which links the neighborhood to Brooklyn Centre and Ohio City attractions. *5 min. from downtown*

Car-Free in Cleveland

WEST PARK

The far west end of Cleveland is often referred to as West Park. The separation of residential and commercial districts makes West Park the most suburban neighborhood of Cleveland. West Park residents have farther to bike or walk to the store, and have few transit options. Still, West Park offers several stations on the Red Line (66X/66S): Triskett, West Park, and Puritas/W. 150th Street, each of which have large Park-n-Ride lots and direct bus connections. Buses serving West Park include RTA's 18, 22, 44, 46, 69, 70, 75X, 78, 50, 83, 86, and 98 routes.
15-40 min. from downtown

EAST SIDE SUBURBS

Cleveland's eastern suburbs are like a big city in themselves, in that they contain older, historic neighborhoods, with a great diversity among their residents. The commercial districts are "on the sidewalk" and, in most cases, have housing above the stores and restaurants.

This section focuses primarily, though not solely, on the most transit-accessible eastern suburbs. It should be noted that trip times for eastern suburbs other than Shaker Heights under-estimate night and weekend trip times from downtown, because most night and weekend buses to the eastern suburbs require you to take the Rapid to University Circle or Windermere and transfer to a bus. Weekday bus trips (preceding the evening hours) run direct to downtown.

BEACHWOOD

Walking and biking in Beachwood can be difficult, mostly due to its traffic and the segregation of residential and retail districts. One of the largest suburban "satellite downtowns" is in Beachwood, located along Chagrin Boulevard (RTA 5 bus), just east of Green Road (RTA 34 bus). Beachwood Place Mall and nearby La Place on Cedar Road are served by the 32 and 94 buses. The Green Line Rapid/67AX terminus at Green Road and Shaker Boulevard and the Blue Line/67X stop at Van Aken and Warrensville Center Roads are both just a block or two from the Beachwood/Shaker Heights boundary.
25-60 min. from downtown

BEDFORD & BEDFORD HEIGHTS

Bedford has an historic business district lining Broadway Avenue, which is a pleasant place to walk while shopping. Broadway has frequent bus service, provided by the 76 and 90X buses. Bedford Heights is a newer, less walkable suburban community. Its bus service is limited to the 41A/41C buses linking Solon to East Cleveland and 802/southeast circulator which serves Bedford and Bedford Heights and Maple Heights.
40-55 min. from downtown

Places to see and things to do

BRATENAHL

The lakefront community of Bratenahl, between E. 85th and E. 140th streets, is an independent municipality that is primarily residential. Bus service is offered by the 39BX, running from downtown Cleveland to Euclid's shopping districts.   *10-15 min. from downtown*

CHAGRIN FALLS

This 19th century farming community has been preserved and improved by strong planning and development controls. When architects talk about trying to restore "Main Street U.S.A." to American towns and suburbs, they are thinking of places like Chagrin Falls. Pedestrian and bicycle access is enjoyable here, and bus service is available on RTA's 5 route to the Blue Line/67X Rapid station at Warrensville Center Road.   *45 min. from downtown*

CLEVELAND HEIGHTS

Outside of the City of Cleveland, Cleveland Heights and Lakewood may be the easiest cities in the region in which to go car-free. Cleveland Heights is very similar to Shaker Heights, in terms of it being pedestrian - transit-, and bicycle-oriented. However, Cleveland Heights has a wider variety of housing options, and has more commercial land intermixed with housing, making it very easy to walk or ride a bike to satisfy your shopping or nightlife needs.

Neighborhoods in Cleveland Heights include:

• Coventry Village is located along Coventry Road between Mayfield Road and Euclid Heights Boulevard. It is easily Greater Cleveland's most Bohemian area, with fascinating bookstores, restaurants, natural-food shops, stores with unique themes, and theaters. Two major east-west bus routes serve Coventry: the 7 and 9 buses. However, there are no north-south buses, and late-night bus service is limited.

• Cedar/Lee, the neighborhood surrounding the intersection of Cedar and Lee Roads is a terrific place to walk, with decent transit access, particularly along Cedar Road (32 buses) and Lee Road (40 bus). The most notable landmark in this neighborhood is the Cedar-Lee Theater, which shows many foreign films.

• Cedar/Fairmount, at the merging of Cedar Road and Fairmount Boulevard, has a number of beautiful old apartment buildings and the old Alcazar Hotel on Surrey Road, plus several restaurants and shops. The major bus routes serving this neighborhood are the 32 and 94. The 7 bus runs along the northern edge of the area, on Euclid Heights Boulevard.   *20-40 min. from downtown*

Car-Free in Cleveland

EAST CLEVELAND
Like most of Cleveland's pre-World War II suburbs, East Cleveland is a pedestrian-oriented, transit-oriented community. The two easternmost Red Line stations, Superior Avenue and Windermere (both recently rebuilt from the ground up), are located here. In addition, East Cleveland is also served by numerous buses, including the 4, 6, 30, 36, 37, 40, and 41. The 6 route offers 24-hour service west to downtown, and late-evening service available on most of the other routes. *20 min. from downtown*

EUCLID
Euclid can boast excellent transit service, especially to and from downtown Cleveland. Buses to Euclid include the 39 routes (most of which run via Lake Shore Boulevard), the 1 (St. Clair), and the 239 (Park-n-Ride flyer). North-south buses include the 30 (Lake Shore/E. 140th), 34 (E. 200th), 37 (E. 185th), 73 (E. 222nd) and 94 (E. 250th) buses. The Euclid Community Circulator/806 links all of the suburb's bus routes, the Park-n-Ride lot, plus most major shopping centers, schools, and medical facilities. *20-45 min. from downtown*

GARFIELD HEIGHTS & MAPLE HEIGHTS
These first-ring suburbs are fairly typical of communities built during the 1950s. Pedestrian-oriented business districts exist along Turney Road in Garfield Heights and Broadway Avenue in Maple Heights. Numerous buses serve Garfield Heights, including the 10, 44, 48X, 76F, 76X, 88X, and 90X. Except for the 10, 44, and 48X, all of these routes continue on to serve Maple Heights. Other routes serving Maple Heights are the 40 and 802/Southeast circulator. *30-50 min. from downtown*

LYNDHURST, MAYFIELD HEIGHTS, HIGHLAND HEIGHTS & RICHMOND HEIGHTS
These communities have limited transit service. Mayfield Road is served by frequent bus service on the 9X and 9F routes. A branch route, the 9BX, runs from downtown Cleveland, down Anderson and Richmond Roads to Richmond Mall. A branch of the 9X runs down Richmond and Ridgebury Boulevard through Highland Heights. Also, serving Richmond and Highland Heights are the 7 and 94 routes. *40-70 min. from downtown*

NORTH RANDALL & WARRENSVILLE HEIGHTS
North Randall has fewer than 5,000 residents, but is served well by transit due to the community being home to Randall Park Mall and other retail. The mall is a transit hub for the 15, 19, 41 and 441

Places to see and things to do

(summers only, to Sea World/Geauga Lake parks) routes.
Warrensville Heights is a mostly suburban community served by the 14, 15, 41, and 441 (summers only, to Sea World/Geauga Lake parks) routes. *40-50 min. from downtown*

SHAKER HEIGHTS

Shaker Heights is one of the most transit-accessible of the eastern suburbs. It also offers wide boulevards that make it a pleasure for safe, scenic bicycle riding. Shaker Heights was built in the 1920s as a planned residential community by the Van Sweringen brothers, who linked the community to downtown via two Rapid transit rail lines. Both the Blue (67X) and Green (67AX) lines extend through Shaker Heights and terminate near its eastern limit, just a few blocks west of the Beachwood/Shaker Heights boundary. The Green Line runs down Shaker Boulevard, while the Blue Line runs in the median of Van Aken Boulevard. Shaker Heights is also served by numerous north-south buses, including the 37, 40, and 41A/C. In addition, the 5, 14, and 94 buses run east-west. *12-25 min. from downtown*

SOLON

This suburb is known for its housing subdivisions, strip shopping centers, parking areas, and traffic. Like most new, low-density suburbs, Solon does not have much transit service. It does have the 41A/41C buses down Aurora Road and RTA's 441 buses (summers only through Solon to the Sea World/Geauga Lake amusement parks). *50-70 min. from downtown*

SOUTH EUCLID & UNIVERSITY HEIGHTS

University Heights, the home to John Carroll University, and South Euclid both have diverse residential and commercial areas. These communities are served by the north-south 34 and 41A/C buses, as well as the east-west 32 buses. The 7 and 9 buses serve South Euclid while the 37 and 94 buses serve University Heights. In addition, most of University Heights is within walking distance of the Green Line's Shaker Blvd. stops. *30-45 min. from downtown*

THE WESTERN SUBURBS
BEREA

Berea is home to Baldwin-Wallace College and is the site of the Cuyahoga County Fairgrounds. The city dates from the 1840s and is full of historic structures in a pedestrian-friendly setting. Limited bus service is offered by RTA's 68, 86, 86F, and 89 routes. *30-45 min. from downtown*

FAIRVIEW PARK

Fairview Park has a stable commercial district along Lorain Road and a large mall (Westgate Mall). It is a community that is somewhat pedestrian friendly. Bus service includes the 22, 75 and 96F along Lorain Road, with the 22, 25, 55NX, 55SX 808/Westshore circulator and 87F buses serving the Westgate Transit Center on Center Ridge Road, just west of W. 210th Street and Westgate Mall.   *25-40 min. from downtown*

INDEPENDENCE & NORTH OLMSTED

Independence and North Olmsted have enough office space to qualify as satellite downtowns (or, in planning jargon, "Edge Cities"). Because of its larger population and the presence of Great Northern Mall, North Olmsted has better bus service. There is the 63F, 64F, 75X, 75F, 87F, 89 and 96F buses, all of which focus on the mall. Independence's bus service is limited to the 44 east-west bus and the 77F bus (linking downtown Cleveland to a connection at Brecksville with Akron Metro buses).   *20-40 min. from downtown*

LAKEWOOD

Lakewood is a city where one can easily prosper without a car. Its population density of 12,000 people per square mile is higher than in Chicago or Philadelphia. As with Cleveland Heights, Lakewood contains a number of identifiable neighborhoods that one would normally find in a large city like Cleveland, including:

Gold Coast: This area is characterized by high-rise apartments and condos, plus classic single-family homes. It is served by the 46F, and 55 buses on Clifton. The 50 and 75X buses run north-south on W. 117th Street to the West 117th/Madison Red Line (66X) Rapid station and beyond. The Lakewood Circulator/804 links the Gold Coast to all of Lakewood, plus the Rapid system.

Downtown Lakewood: Truly a downtown, this is one of the largest employment centers in Greater Cleveland. Several bus routes serve downtown Lakewood, including the 24-hour 326 route plus the 86, and 70 and the Lakewood Circulator/804.

West End: This area, next to the Rocky River and Cleveland Metroparks, offers a mix of new and old apartment buildings and single-family homes, plus a number of restaurants and nightclubs. Transit service to the West End is provided by the 24-hour 326 bus and the 55 buses along Sloan Avenue and Clifton Road. The Lakewood Community Circulator/804 also serves the West End.

Bird Town: Intersecting streets named Quail, Robin, and Lark gave this community its name. It is a short walk to the W. 117th/Madison Red Line (66X/66S) Rapid station. Bird Town is served by the 25 buses along Madison and the Lakewood Circulator/804.   *15-35 min. from downtown*

Places to see and things to do

PARMA

Parma is Cleveland's largest suburb, with about 85,000 residents. Pedestrian-friendly areas are concentrated in the older commercial districts along Pearl and Ridge Roads. Frequent bus service on Pearl is offered by the 51X. To some, a large cluster of apartment buildings and townhouses near Parmatown Mall can offer a car-free lifestyle. Parmatown Mall is a major bus hub, served by the 20 A/B, 23, 45, 68, and 79 buses. All those buses head to downtown Cleveland, except for the 45 (to Lakewood's Gold Coast) and the 68 (to Berea and to Great Northern Mall in North Olmsted).
20-40 min. from downtown

ROCKY RIVER & BAY VILLAGE

Rocky River and Bay Village, like Lakewood, are older lakefront suburbs. Because of development densities and the amount of transit service, it is easier to go car-free in Rocky River, especially if you live near the old Detroit Road shopping district, close to Lakewood and the western terminus of the 24-hour 326 buses. Buses serving both Rocky River and Bay Village are the 31X, 55CX, 55CF and 55X. Serving Rocky River but not Bay Village are the 326, 22, 25, 46, 55NX, 55SX, 55X, 65F, 87F, 808/Westshore circulator and 96F buses.

> **BY THE WAY**
>
> You can easily travel without a car from Cleveland to many Northeast Ohio colleges: Cleveland State University, the University of Akron, Baldwin-Wallace College, John Carroll University, Cuyahoga Community College (all three campuses), Kent State University, Lakeland Community College, Lake Erie College, Lorain County Community College, Oberlin College, Ursuline College, and others!

25-50 min. from downtown

STRONGSVILLE & WESTLAKE

Westlake and Strongsville are newly-minted, fast-growing suburbs. Westlake's transit service is fairly decent for a newer, outer-edge suburb. Both suburbs have new Park-n-Ride lots with frequent rush-hour buses on the freeways to downtown Cleveland. Westlake is served by the 46, 55NX and 55SX, 65F, 87F, 808/Westshore circulator and 246 buses (the latter serving the Park-n-Ride). Strongsville is served by the 51X, 51F, 86, 89, 151, 251 and 451 buses. The last three buses are flyer buses which use Interstate 71. The 51X and 251 buses serve the Strongsville Park-n-Ride.
35-60 min. from downtown

73

Car-Free in Cleveland

OTHER DESTINATIONS IN GREATER CLEVELAND

GREATER CLEVELAND COLLEGES & UNIVERSITIES

Akron University, 302 Buchtel Common, Akron. ☎330-972-7111.
🚌 Served by many Akron METRO bus routes, including the X61/Cleveland, X77/Akron-Canton Airport, 101/Richfield, 102/Northfield, 103/Glen Willow-Twinsburg-Hudson, 110/Green-Springfield.

Baldwin Wallace College, 275 Eastland Rd., Berea. ☎440-826-2424.
🚌 Served by RTA 68, 86 and 89 buses.

Borromeo Seminary, 28700 Euclid Ave., Wickcliffe. ☎440-943-7600.
🚌 Served by RTA 49F and LAKETRAN 2 buses.

Bryant & Stratton College Downtown Campus, 1700 E. 13th Street, Cleveland. ☎216-771-1700. 🚌 On or near numerous downtown RTA, Akron METRO, and LAKETRAN bus routes. Also about a half-mile from the 🚌 Tower City Rapid station (RTA Red/66X/66S, Blue/67X, and Green/67AX lines) and North Coast Rapid station (RTA Blue/67X and Green/67AX lines).

Bryant & Stratton College East Side Campus, 691 Richmond Rd., Richmond Heights. ☎440-461-3151. 🚌 In the Richmond Mall, served by RTA 7, 9BX, 73 and 94 buses.

Bryant & Stratton College West Side Campus, 12955 Snow Rd., Parma. ☎216-265-3151. 🚌 Served by RTA 44 and 83 buses.

Capital University, 1320 Sumner Court, Cleveland. ☎216-781-0228. 🚌 Near 14th & Sumner, on RTA 15, 76F, 77F, and 97F, plus Akron METRO 60 and 61 bus routes. Also a 3/4 mile walk from Tower City Rapid station (RTA 66X, 66S, 67X, 67AX) and LAKETRAN bus routes.

Case Western Reserve University, 10900 Euclid Ave., Cleveland. ☎216-368-2000. 🚌 Served by RTA 6 and 9 buses. Also, some CWRU buildings are virtually across the street from the University Circle Rapid station (RTA Red Line/66X).

Cleveland College of Jewish Studies, 26500 Shaker Blvd., Beachwood. ☎ 216-464-4050. 🚌 About 1 mile east of the Green Road Rapid station (RTA Green/67AX Line), or 1/2 mile from Fairmount and Richmond (served by RTA 94 bus).

Cleveland Institute of Art, 11141 East Blvd., Cleveland. ☎216-421-7000.
🚌 Take RTA 6 and 9 buses up Euclid Ave., then walk north on East Blvd. Also, take Rapid (RTA Red Line/66X) to University Circle station, walk north on Martin Luther King to Euclid, then go to East Blvd. as suggested above. The 7F bus serves Euclid during rush hours.

Places to see and things to do

Cleveland Institute of Music, 11021 East Blvd., Cleveland. 216-791-5000. 🚌 Same as Cleveland Institute of Art, but walk a block further north up East Blvd.

Cleveland State University, East 24th St. & Euclid Avenue, Cleveland. ☎216-687-2000. 🚌 Euclid Avenue, site of many CSU buildings, is directly on RTA 6, 9 and Outer Loop. Other RTA, Akron METRO and LAKETRAN downtown Cleveland buses serve nearby blocks, or serve the university's western fringe.

Cuyahoga Community College Main Campus, 2900 Community College Avenue, Cleveland. ☎216-987-4000. 🚌 1/4 mile west of the E. 34th St. Rapid station (RTA Red/66X, Blue/67X and Green/67AX lines). In addition, the campus is directly served by RTA 14, 15, 25, 33, 35 and Outer Loop buses. Also, RTA 90X runs 1/4 mile south and west of the campus.

Cuyahoga Community College East Side Campus, 4250 Richmond Road, Highland Hills. ☎ 216-987-2000. 🚌 Served by RTA 14 bus.

Cuyahoga Community College West Side Campus, 11000 W. Pleasant Valley Rd., Parma. ☎ 216-987-5000. 🚌 Served by RTA 68 and 79 buses.

David N. Myers College, formerly Dyke College, 112 Prospect Ave., Cleveland. ☎ 216-696-9000. 🚌 Four blocks east of Tower City Rapid station (RTA Red/66X/66S, Blue/67X, and Green/67AX) and a short walk from almost all RTA, Akron METRO, and LAKETRAN downtown Cleveland buses.

Hiram College, At Ohio routes 700 and 82, Hiram. ☎330-569-3211. 🚌 No regular route transit service is available to this town, which is home to Hiram College. You can try reserving a Portage Area Regional Transportation Authority (PARTA) "Dial-A-Ride" bus from Solon, which is the closest city to Hiram that is served by RTA (#41 bus).

John Carroll University, 20700 N. Park Blvd., University Heights. ☎216-397-1886. 🚌 Served by RTA 32WX, 41A, 41C, and 94 buses. Also 1/3-mile north of Warrensville Rapid station (RTA Green/67AX Line).

Kent State University, Student Center-Risman Drive, Kent. ☎330-672-2121. 🚌 Served by buses within Kent, plus from Akron, Cleveland, East Liverpool, Ravenna, Stow, Twin Lakes, and Warren.

Lake Erie College, 391 West Washington Street, Painesville. ☎440-352-3361. 🚌 Served by LAKETRAN #

Lakeland Community College, 7700 Clocktower Drive, Kirtland. ☎440-953-7000. 🚌 Served by LAKETRAN #1 bus and #11 Cleveland Flyer bus. Take RTA 39 bus to Shoregate, connect to LAKETRAN #3 or #6 buses to Great Lakes Mall, then connect to LAKETRAN #1 bus to Lakeland Community College.

Lorain County Community College, 1005 North Abbe Road, Elyria. ☎ 440-365-5222. 🚌 Served by Lorain County Transit's "North Ridgeville" route,

75

Car-Free in Cleveland

which connects with RTA's 75X bus at the county line. Also served by LCT's "East Loop" bus, which connects at Avon Lake Ford Plant with RTA 31X.

Maranatha Bible College, 4930 Lee Rd., Cleveland. ☎ 216-663-9773. 🚌 Served by RTA 40 bus.

McCreary Institute for African American Religious Studies, 1508 E. 71st St., Cleveland. ☎ 216-431-1989. 🚌 Several blocks south of Wade Park Ave. (on RTA 4 route). And several blocks north of Hough (on RTA 38 route).

Notre Dame College, 4545 College Rd., South Euclid. ☎ 216-381-1680. 🚌 Served by RTA 34 bus, and several blocks north of Cedar, served by RTA 32CX and 32SX buses.

Oberlin College, 173 West Lorain Street, Oberlin. ☎ 440-775-8121. 🚌 Served by Lorain County Transit's daily "Lorain-Elyria-Oberlin" route. Connect to LCT Oberlin buses via Greyhound at Elyria Greyound depot. Or, take RTA 75X to LCT "North Ridgeville" bus, then connect in Elyria to LCT Oberlin, or take RTA 31X to LCT "East Loop" bus, and connect at Lorain or Elyria to Oberlin bus.

Ohio College of Podiatric Medicine, 10515 Carnegie Ave., Cleveland. ☎216-231-3300. 🚌 Just south of Euclid (served by RTA 6 and 9 buses) and just east of E. 105th (served by RTA 10 bus).

Telshe Yeshiva College, 28400 Euclid Ave., Euclid. ☎ 216-943-5300. 🚌 Served by RTA 49F bus and LAKETRAN 2 bus.

Ursuline College, 2550 Lander Rd., Pepper Pike. ☎ 440-449-4200. 🚌 Served by some RTA 32CX and 32SX buses.

Yavne College for Women, 1970 S. Taylor Rd., Cleveland Heights. ☎216-371-8566. 🚌 Served by RTA 37 bus, and a few blocks north of Cedar (served by RTA 32 buses).

GREATER CLEVELAND HOSPITALS

Campus Hospital of Cleveland, 18120 Puritas Ave., Cleveland. ☎ 216-476-0222. 🚌 On RTA 78 bus route. Also a block west of Rocky River Dr., and RTA 86 bus.

Cleveland Clinic Foundation, 9500 Euclid Ave., Cleveland. ☎ 216-444-2200. 🚌 Served by RTA 6, 7F and 9 buses.

Cleveland Clinic Independence, 5005 Rockside Rd., Independence. ☎ 216-520-3700. 🚌 Served by RTA 44 bus.

Cleveland Clinic Lakewood, 16215 Madison Ave., ☎ 216-521-4400 FServed by RTA 25, 65X and 804.

Cleveland Clinic Solon, 29800 Bainbridge Rd., Solon. ☎ 440-519-6800. F A block north of Aurora Rd., served by RTA 41A, 41C and, in summer only, RTA 441 buses.

Places to see and things to do

Cleveland Clinic Westlake, 30033 Clemens Rd., Westlake. ☎ 440-899-5555. 🚌 1/3 mile north of Detroit Rd., served by RTA 46 and 55X buses.

Cleveland Clinic Willoughby Hills, 2570 SOM Center Rd., Willoughby Hills. ☎ 216-943-2500. 🚌 Served by LAKETRAN #4 bus.

Deaconess Hospital of Cleveland, 4229 Pearl Rd., Cleveland. ☎ 216-459-6300. 🚌 Served by RTA 20, 20A, 21X, 35, and 51X buses.

Fairview Hospital, 18101 Lorain Ave., Cleveland. ☎ 216-476-7000. 🚌 Served by RTA 22 and 75X buses, with RTA 86 bus 1/3-mile east of hospital.

Grace Hospital, 2307 W. 14th St., Cleveland. ☎ 216-687-1500. 🚌 Served by RTA 81 bus and Tremont Circulator/RTA 807.

Health Hill Hospital For Children, 2801 Martin Luther King, Jr. Drive, Cleveland. ☎ 216-721-5400. 🚌 Go to E. 116th Rapid station (RTA Blue/67X and Green/67AX lines), then walk several blocks west to Martin Luther King, then walk a block or so south.

Lakewood Hospital, 14519 Detroit Ave., Lakewood. ☎ 216-521-4200. 🚌 Served by RTA 326 and 804 buses, with RTA 86 bus two blocks west, and RTA 70 bus six blocks east.

Lutheran Hospital, 1730 West 25th St., Cleveland. ☎ 216-696-4300. 🚌 Take RTA 20, 20A, 20B, 21X, and 51X buses to W. 25th and Franklin. Alternatively, take Rapid to W. 25th/Ohio City Rapid station (RTA Red Line/66X), walk one block west on Lorain and six blocks north on W. 25th to Franklin.

Marymount Hospital, 12300 McCracken Rd., Garfield Heights. ☎ 216-581-0500. 🚌 Served by RTA 10, 48, and 88X buses.

Meridia Euclid Hospital, 18901 Lake Shore Blvd., Euclid. ☎ 216-531-9000. 🚌 Served by RTA 30, 34, 37, and 39 buses routes.

Meridia Hillcrest Hospital, 6780 Mayfield Rd., Mayfield Heights. ☎ 440-449-4500. 🚌 Served by RTA 7 and 9 buses.

Meridia Huron Hospital, 13951 Terrace Rd., East Cleveland. ☎ 216-761-3300. 🚌 Served by RTA 36 bus, or take RTA 6, 9 and 40 buses, then walk a couple of blocks along Terrace to the hospital. Also, the Superior Rapid station (RTA Red Line/66X) is seven blocks away, also served by RTA 36 bus.

Meridia South Pointe Hospital, 4110 Warrensville Center Rd., Warrensville Heights. ☎216-491-6000. 🚌 Served by RTA 15, 41A and 41C in summer only, RTA 441 buses. Also several blocks south of Harvard, served by RTA 14 bus route.

MetroHealth Medical Center, 2500 MetroHealth Drive, Cleveland. ☎ 216-778-7800. 🚌 Served by RTA 81 bus, while 20, 20A, 20B, 21X, 35, and 51X bus routes are one block west on W. 25th.

Car-Free in Cleveland

PHS Mt. Sinai Medical Campus, 26900 Cedar Rd., Beachwood. ☎ 216-595-2500. 🚌 Served by RTA 4, 10, 38, 48 and 50 buses, plus from September to May it is served by KSU's campus bus service from Kent 32CX, 32SX and 94 buses.

PHS Mt. Sinai Medical Center - University Circle, 1 Mt. Sinai Drive, Cleveland. ☎ 216-421-4000. 🚌 Served by RTA

PHS Mt. Sinai Medical Center East, 27100 Chardon Rd., Richmond Heights. ☎ 216-585-6500. 🚌 Served by RTA 94 bus.

Parma Community General Hospital, 7007 Powers Blvd., Parma. ☎ 440-888-1800. 🚌 Served by RTA 20A, 20B, 45, 68 and 79 buses.

St. Michael Hospital, 5163 Broadway, Cleveland. ☎ 216-429-8000. 🚌 Served by RTA 19, 76X, 88X, 90X, and 97X buses.

St. John West Shore Hospital, 29000 Center Ridge Rd., Westlake. ☎ 440-835-8000. 🚌 Served by RTA 42, 55SX and 65F buses.

St. Luke's Medical Center, 11311 Shaker Blvd., Cleveland. ☎ 216-368-7000. 🚌 Served by RTA 35 bus, and just three blocks west of E. 116th Rapid station (RTA Blue/67X and Green/67AX lines). Also, three blocks west of RTA 50 bus, three blocks south of 25W bus, and three blocks north of 25B bus.

St. Vincent Charity Hospital, 2351 E. 22nd St., Cleveland. ☎ 216-861-6200. 🚌 Served by RTA 14, 15, 90X, and Outer Loop buses.

Southwest General Health Center, 18697 E. Bagley Rd., Middleburg Heights. ☎ 440-816-8000. 🚌 Served by 68, 86F and 89 buses.

University Hospitals of Cleveland, 11100 Euclid Ave., Cleveland. ☎ 216-844-1000. 🚌 Take RTA 6, 7F, 9, 48, 48A, and 50 buses. Hospital is several blocks north of the University Circle Rapid station (Red Line/66X), which is also served by RTA 6A, 7X, 8, 32CX, 32SX and 94 buses.

GREATER CLEVELAND MUSEUMS & HISTORICAL SOCIETIES

African American Museum, 1765 Crawford Rd., Cleveland. ☎ 216-791-1700. 🚌 Take RTA 38 bus on Hough to Crawford (near E. 86th), and walk a block or so west. Or take 6 and 9 buses to Euclid and E. 85th and walk a couple of blocks north to Crawford.

Cleveland Botanical Garden, 11030 East Blvd., Cleveland. ☎ 216-721-1600. 🚌 Take RTA 6, 9, 48, 48A, and 50 buses, and KSU/Campus Bus-Cleveland (doesn't run in summer) to Euclid and East Blvd., then walk north on East Blvd.

Cleveland Museum of Art, 11150 East Blvd., Cleveland. ☎ 216-421-7340. 🚌 Take RTA 6, 9, 48, 48A, and 50 buses, and KSU/Campus Bus-Cleveland (doesn't run in summer), then walk north on East Blvd.

Places to see and things to do

Cleveland Museum of Natural History, 1 Wade Oval, Cleveland. ☎ 216-231-4600. 🚌 Same as Botanical Garden (above) but walk further north until you encounter Wade Oval.

The National Cleveland-Style Polka Hall of Fame, 291 E. 222nd St., Euclid. ☎ 216-261-3263. 🚌 Take RTA 39 buses to Lake Shore and walk down E. 222 to Euclid Shore Civic Centre. If going north from eastern suburbs, take 73 bus up E. 222nd.

Great Lakes Science Center, 601 Erieside at North Coast Harbor, Cleveland. ☎ 216-694-2000. 🚌 Across the Shoreway from the North Coast Rapid station (RTA Blue/67X and Green/67AX lines). Alternatively, take 39 buses to North Coast Rapid station, or other downtown buses to E. 9th and walk north past Shoreway.

The Health Museum of Cleveland, 9811 Euclid Ave., Cleveland. ☎ 216-231-5010. 🚌 Take 6 and 9 buses up Euclid. Also nine blocks west of RTA 2 bus.

Inventure Place/National Inventors Hall of Fame, 221 South Broadway St., Akron. ☎ 330-762-4463. 🚌 Served by many Akron METRO bus routes, including the X61/Cleveland, X77/Akron-Canton Airport, 101/Richfield, 102/Northfield, 103/Glen Willow-Twinsburg-Hudson, 110/Green-Springfield.

NASA Glenn Research Center and Visitor Center, 21000 Brookpark Rd., Cleveland. ☎ 216-433-2001. 🚌 Served by RTA 75F and 78 buses.

Rainbow Children's Museum, 10730 Euclid Ave., Cleveland. ☎ 216-791-7114. 🚌 Take RTA 6, 9, 48, 48A, and 50 buses, and KSU/Campus Bus-Cleveland (doesn't run in summer).

Rock and Roll Hall of Fame & Museum, One Key Plaza, Cleveland. ☎ 216-781-ROCK. 🚌 Across Shoreway from North Coast Rapid station (RTA Blue/67X and Green/67AX lines). Or take 39 bus to North Coast Rapid station, or other downtown buses to E. 9th and walk north of Shoreway.

Western Reserve Historical Society/Crawford Auto-Aviation Museum, 10825 East Blvd., Cleveland. ☎ 216-721-5722. 🚌 Take RTA 6, 9, 48, 48A, and 50 buses, and KSU/Campus Bus-Cleveland (doesn't run in summer), then walk north on East Boulevard.

GREATER CLEVELAND SHOPPING CENTERS

The Arcade, 401 Euclid Ave., Cleveland (61 stores). ☎ 216-621-8500. 🚌 Two blocks east of Tower City Rapid station (RTA Red/66X/66S, Blue/67X and Green/67AX lines). Directly served by dozens of RTA, Akron METRO and LAKETRAN downtown bus routes.

Asia Plaza, 2999 Payne Ave., Cleveland (30 shops). ☎ 216-241-3553. 🚌 Directly served by RTA 4 and 38 bus routes. Several blocks south of RTA 1 and 326 buses.

Car-Free in Cleveland

Beachwood Place, 26300 Cedar Rd., Beachwood (102 stores). ☎ 216-464-9460. 🚌 Served by RTA 32CX, 32SX, and 94 buses. Next door is La Place Fashion Centre, with 30 stores.

Euclid Square Mall, Babbitt Rd. & E. 260th St., Euclid (118 stores). ☎ 216-731-6899. 🚌 Served by RTA 1, 39, 94 buses and 808/Westshore circulator.

The Galleria At Erieview, 1301 E. 9th St., Cleveland (65 stores). ☎ 216-621-9999. 🚌 2 blocks south of North Coast Rapid station (RTA Blue/67X and Green 67/AX lines). Directly served by RTA 1, 8, 11, 15, 19, 33, 39, 77F, 81, 90X buses and LAKETRAN 10, 12, 13 buses–and within a few blocks of numerous other downtown Cleveland RTA and Akron METRO bus routes.

Golden Gate Shopping Center, Mayfield Rd. & I-271, Mayfield Heights (43 stores). 🚌 Served by RTA 9 bus.

Great Lakes Mall, 7850 Mentor Ave., Mentor (100 stores). ☎ 440-255-6900. 🚌 Served by LAKETRAN routes 1, 2, 3 and 6.

Great Northern Mall, Great Northern Blvd. & I-480, North Olmsted (155 stores). ☎ 440-734-6300. 🚌 Served by RTA 42, 53, 63F, 64F, 75X, 75F, 87F, 89 and 96F buses.

Parmatown Mall, W. Ridgewood Dr. & Ridge Rd., Parma (170 stores). ☎ 440-885-2090. 🚌 Served by RTA 20A, 20B, 23, 45, 68 and 79 buses.

Pavilion Shopping Center, 24055 Chagrin Blvd., Beachwood. ☎ 216-292-7765. 🚌 Served by RTA 5 and 34 buses.

Randall Park Mall, Warrensville Center Rd. & SR 43, North Randall (192 stores). ☎ 216-663-1250. 🚌 Take RTA 15, 19, 34, 41 buses and 802/Westshore circulator.

Richmond Mall, 691 Richmond Rd, Richmond Heights (98 stores). ☎ 440-449-3200. 🚌 Served by RTA 7, 9BX, 73 and 94 buses.

Severance Town Center, 3640 Mayfield Rd., Cleveland Heights (85 stores).☎ 216-381-7323. 🚌 Served RTA 9, 37 and 41S buses.

Shaker Square, N. Moreland & Shaker Blvd., Cleveland (36 stores). ☎ 216-991-8700. 🚌 Directly served by Shaker Square Rapid station (RTA Blue/67X and Green/67AX lines). Also served by RTA 25 and 48 buses and KSU/Campus Bus-Cleveland (doesn't run in summer).

Shaker Town Center, 16500-17400 Chagrin Blvd., Shaker Heights (42 stores). 🚌 One block south of Lee Road Rapid station (RTA Blue/67X Line). Also served by RTA 14 and 40 buses

Shoregate Shopping Center, E. 305th St. & Lakeshore Blvd., Willowick (53 stores). ☎ 440-944-9266. 🚌 Served by RTA 39 and 43F, plus LAKE-TRAN 2, 3 and 6 buses.

Places to see and things to do

Southgate USA, 20990 Libby Rd., Maple Heights (165 stores). ☎ 216-662-8451. 🚍 Served by RTA 41A, 41C, 76, 90X, 97F buses and 802/Westshore circulator.

Southland Shopping Center, Pearl Rd. & W. 130th St., Middleburg Heights (100 stores). ☎ 216-464-5550. 🚍 Served by RTA 51X, 351, 70 and 83 buses.

Southpark Center, Royalton & Howe roads, Strongsville (165 stores). ☎ 440-238-9000. 🚍 Served by RTA 51 and 89 buses.

The Avenue at Tower City Center, 230 Huron Rd., behind Public Square, Cleveland (96 stores). ☎ 216-771-0333. 🚍 At Tower City Rapid station (RTA Red/66X/66S, Blue/67X and Green/67AX lines), and served by a majority of RTA, Akron METRO and LAKETRAN downtown Cleveland buses.

Westgate Mall, W. 210th St. & Center Ridge Rd., Fairview Park (97 stores). ☎ 440-333-8334. 🚍 Served by RTA 22, 25, 55NX, 87F, 326 buses and 808/Westshore circulator.

NIGHTLIFE DISTRICTS

Nightlife Districts offer multiple nightclubs, theaters, and restaurants in a walkable setting. See *Scene Magazine*, *The Cleveland Free Times*, and the *Plain Dealer* Friday Magazine for details about certain establishments offering live music, as well as comedy club acts, billiard clubs, poetry readings, and other special appearances.

Cedar-Lee, East Side - Cedar & Lee roads, Cleveland Heights. 🚍 Served by RTA 32 buses east-west on Cedar and RTA 40 bus north-south on Lee.

Coventry Village, East Side - Coventry Rd., between Euclid Heights Blvd. & Mayfield Rd., Cleveland Heights. 🚍 Served by RTA 7 buses. Or, take 9 bus up Mayfield to Coventry.

Downtown Lakewood, West Side - Detroit & Warren Rds., Lakewood. 🚍 Take RTA 326 bus on Detroit Ave., or 86 bus on Warren Rd.

The Flats, Downtown - East and West banks of Cuyahoga River, near Lake Erie, Cleveland. 🚍 Directly served by Flats East Bank and Settlers Landing Rapid stations (RTA Blue/67X and Green/67AX lines). Cross river using water taxis (summers only). Or, walk 4-10 blocks northwest of Public Square, which is served by dozens of downtown bus and rapid routes.

Gateway, Downtown - From Jacobs Field north to Euclid Ave., Cleveland. 🚍 Walk several blocks east (use Gateway Walkway in foul weather) from Tower City Rapid station (RTA Red/66X/66S, Blue/67X, and Green/67AX lines). Or, take one of dozens of RTA, Akron METRO and LAKETRAN buses which serve the downtown area and special events at Gateway.

Little Italy-Murray Hill, East Side - Mayfield and Murray Hill roads, Cleveland. 🚍 Directly served by 9 buses, or walk from University Circle or Euclid-E. 120 Rapid stations served by RTA Red Line/66X and 4, 6, 7, 8, 32, 48, 50 and 94 buses.

Car-Free in Cleveland

Madison Village, West Side - Madison Ave., between Bunts and Hilliard Roads, Lakewood. 🚌 Take RTA 25, 65X, 70, and 86 buses.

Ohio City, West Side - North of Lorain Ave. south of Detroit Ave., west of W. 25th, east of W. 32nd., Cleveland. 🚌 Served by W. 25th-Ohio City Rapid station (RTA Red Line/66X/66S) or RTA 20, 20A, 20B, 21X, 22, 25, 35, 69, 79, 326, and Tremont Community Circulator 807 buses.

Old World District, East Side - E. 185th, between I-90 and Lake Shore Blvd., Cleveland-Euclid. 🚌 Served by RTA 30, 34, 37 and 39 buses.

Playhouse Square Center, Downtown - Euclid Ave., between E. 14th and E. 17th streets, Cleveland. 🚌 Served by, and within a few blocks of, most downtown Cleveland RTA routes.

Shaker Square, East Side - Shaker Blvd. and North Moreland Blvd., Cleveland. 🚌 Directly served by Shaker Square Rapid station (RTA Blue/67X and Green/67AX lines). Also served by RTA 25 and 48 buses and KSU/Campus Bus-Cleveland (doesn't run in summer).

Tremont, West Side - east of W. 14th, west of W. 7th, north of Starkweather, south of University, Cleveland. 🚌 Take RTA 81 and Tremont Community Circulator 807 bus.

University Circle, East Side - Vicinity of Euclid Ave., between East Blvd. and E. 115th, Cleveland. 🚌 Served by RTA 6, 9, 38, 48, 48A and 50 buses, and KSU/Campus Bus-Cleveland (doesn't run in summer). Also, a few blocks from University Circle Rapid station (RTA Red Line/66X) and RTA 7X, 8, 32 and 94 buses.

Warehouse District, Downtown - West of Ontario, east of the Flats, north of Superior and south of Lakeside., Cleveland. 🚌 Two blocks uphill from Flats East Bank and Settlers Landing Rapid stations (RTA Blue/67X and Blue 67AX lines). Warehouse District is three blocks northwest of Public Square, which is served by dozens of downtown bus and rapid routes.

West Edge-Clifton, West Side - Along Detroit and Clifton roads, between W. 110th and Fry Ave., Cleveland-Lakewood. 🚌 Take RTA 326 bus on Detroit Ave., 31X, 45, 46F and 55 buses on Clifton, or 50 and 75X buses on W. 117th. Or, walk 1/2-mile west of West Boulevard Rapid station (RTA Red Line/66X/66S, and 78 buses).

West End, West Side - Detroit Rd., in the vicinity of Riverside Dr., Lakewood. 🚌 Served by RTA 326 bus. One block east of 55X route.

GREATER CLEVELAND MOVIE THEATERS

Cedar Lee, 2163 Lee Rd. at corner of Cedar and Lee, Cleveland Heights. ☎ 216-321-8232. 🚌 Served by RTA 32 buses on Cedar and 40 bus on Lee.

Centrum Landmark Theatre, 2781 Euclid Heights Blvd., at Coventry and

Places to see and things to do

Euclid Heights, Cleveland Heights. ☎ 216-932-5956. 🚌 Served by RTA 7 bus. Or, take RTA 9 bus to Coventry, and walk several blocks south until you reach Euclid Heights Blvd.

The Cleveland Cinematheque, 11141 East Blvd., Cleveland. ☎ 216-421-7450. 🚌 Take RTA 6, 9, 48, 48A, and 50 buses, or KSU/Campus Bus-Cleveland bus (doesn't run in summer) to East Blvd., then walk several blocks on East Blvd. Or, go to University Circle Rapid station (RTA Red Line/66X, and 8, 7X, 32, 94 buses) walk north on Martin Luther King to Euclid, then go to East Blvd. and walk north.

Colony Theatre, 13116 Shaker Square, Cleveland. ☎ 216-283-6333. 🚌 Half a block south of Shaker Square Rapid station (RTA Blue/67X and Green/67AX lines). Also served by all RTA 25 and 48 buses, and KSU/Campus Bus-Cleveland bus (doesn't run in summer).

Detroit Theatre, 16407 Detroit Rd., Lakewood. ☎ 216-521-2245. 🚌 Served by RTA 326 and Lakewood Circulator/804 buses.

Garfield Mall Movies, 12686 Rockside Rd., Rockside at Turney, Garfield Heights. ☎ 216-662-6155. 🚌 Served by RTA 44, 76, 88X, and 802/Westshore circulator buses.

Great Lakes Mall Movies, 7580 Mentor Ave., Willoughby. ☎ 440-951-3500. 🚌 Served by LAKETRAN routes 1, 2, 3 and 6.

Tower City Center, off Public Square, Cleveland. ☎ 216-621-1172. 🚌 At Tower City Rapid station (RTA Red/66X/66S, Blue/67X, and Green/67AX lines) and dozens of RTA, Akron METRO, and LAKETRAN bus routes.

LakeShore, E. 226th and Lake Shore Blvd., Euclid. ☎ 216-731-1700. 🚌 Served by RTA 39 buses. Also a few blocks east of E. 222nd and Lake Shore (served by RTA 73 bus).

Loews Theatre East 8, Richmond Mall, Richmond Heights. ☎ 440-556-2530. 🚌 Served by RTA 7, 9BX, 73 and 94 buses.

Omnimax Theater, 601 Erieside Ave. (at Great Lakes Science Center), Cleveland. ☎ 216-694-2000. 🚌 Several blocks north of North Coast Rapid station (RTA Blue/67X and Green/67AX lines), RTA 39, 43F and 49F buses, plus LAKETRAN 10, 11, 12 and 13 buses.

Parma Theatre, 5826 Ridge Rd., Ridge at Snow, Parma. ☎ 216-885-0600. 🚌 Take RTA 44, 45, and 79 buses. Also, a couple of long blocks from Pearl/Snow intersection (served by 51X bus).

Parmatown Cinema, 8141 W. Ridgewood Drive, Parma. ☎ 440-884-6406. 🚌 Take RTA 20A, 20B, 23, 45, 68 and 79 buses.

Regal Cinema at Severance Town Centre, Mayfield at Taylor, 3590 Mayfield Rd., Cleveland Heights. ☎ 216-291-1244. 🚌 Served by RTA 9, 37 and 41S buses.

83

Car-Free in Cleveland

Southgate Cinema, 5390 Northfield Road, Northgate at Libby, Maple Heights/Bedford Heights border. ☎ 216-475-3211. 🚌 Take RTA 41A, 41C, 76, 90X and 802/Westshore circulator buses.

Strongsville Cinema, 14720 Pearl, Strongsville. ☎ 440-572-0134. 🚌 Served by RTA 51, 89, 151 and 451 buses.

Westgate Mall, W. 210th and Center Ridge Rd., Rocky River/Fairview Park border. ☎ 440-356-1035. 🚌 Served by RTA 22, 25, 53, 55NX, 55SX, 87F, 326 and 808/Westshore circulator buses.

Westwood Town Center Cinema, 21653 Center Ridge Road, Rocky River. ☎ 440-331-2815. 🚌 Served by RTA 55SX buses. Also a few blocks west of Westgate Transit Center, served by RTA 22, 25, 55NX, 326 and 808/Westshore circulator buses.

Yorktown, Brookpark Rd. at Pearl Rd., Cleveland. ☎ 216-661-6330. 🚌 Take RTA 20B, 51X, 79, and 98 buses to Brookpark and Pearl.

GREATER CLEVELAND THEATERS & PLAYHOUSES

Beck Center for the Cultural Arts, 17801 Detroit Ave., Lakewood. ☎ 216-521-2540. 🚌 Served by RTA 326 and Lakewood Circulator 804 buses.

Blossom Music Center, 1145 West Steels Corners Rd., Cuyahoga Falls. ☎ 330-920-8040. 🚌 *Not accessible by public transportation.*

Clague Playhouse, 1371 Clague Rd., Westlake. ☎ 440-331-0403. 🚌 Take RTA 46 and 55X buses to Clague and Detroit, then walk a couple of blocks south on Clague. Also, the 65 bus has limited service to Clague and Hilliard, just north of this theatre.

The Cleveland Play House, 8500 Euclid Ave., Cleveland. ☎ 216-795-7000. 🚌 Take RTA 6 and 9 buses up Euclid. Also, six blocks east of RTA 2, and eight blocks west of RTA 48 and 48A buses.

Cleveland Public Theatre, 6415 Detroit Ave., Cleveland. ☎ 216-631-2727. 🚌 On RTA 326 routes, and just a block east of the 45 bus.

Dobama Theatre, 1846 Coventry Rd., Cleveland Heights. ☎ 216-932-6838. 🚌 Take the RTA 7 bus to Mayfield/Coventry area. Also, RTA 9 buses stop at Mayfield, just north of this theater.

East Cleveland Theatre, 14108 Euclid Ave., East Cleveland. ☎ 216-851-8721. 🚌 Take RTA 6 bus up Euclid. Or, travel to Windermere Rapid station (RTA Red Line/66X and 30, 36, 41 and some 9 buses) then walk down Euclid to theatre.

Greenbrier Theatre, 6200 Pearl Rd., Parma Heights. ☎ 440-842-4600. 🚌 Served by RTA 51X and 351 buses. Also a couple blocks of Pearl and York, served by RTA 23 bus.

Places to see and things to do

Halle Theatre, 3505 Mayfield Rd., Cleveland Heights. ☎ 216-382-4000 ext. 274. 🚌 Take RTA 9 bus on Mayfield. Or take RTA 37 bus to Mayfield, then walk up Mayfield to Jewish Community Center, which contains theatre.

Karamu House, 2355 E. 89th St., Cleveland. ☎ 216-795-7077. 🚌 Take RTA 35 bus to 89th and Quincy.

Playhouse Square, 1519 Euclid Ave., Cleveland. ☎ 216-241-6000. 🚌 This complex contains the Allen, Hanna, Ohio, State and Palace Theaters. Served by many downtown bus routes, including RTA 6, 7F, 9, 31X, 35, 51, 55, 65, 69, 76F, 77F, 86F, 97F, and Outer Loop routes, also Akron METRO X60, X61 and LAKETRAN 10, 11, 12, 13 buses.

Severance Hall, 11001 Euclid Ave., Cleveland. ☎ 216-231-7300. 🚌 Take RTA 6, 9, 48 and 50 buses

GREATER CLEVELAND METROPARKS

The Cleveland Metroparks system is one of the treasures of Northeast Ohio. Made up of fourteen reservations and the Cleveland Metroparks Zoo, the Metropark system's "Emerald Necklace" of green open spaces surrounding the heart of Greater Cleveland contains over 19,000 acres of recreational opportunities. Though some of the Metroparks are easily accessible by public transit, others are, unfortunately, difficult to reach if you're car-free (see the descriptions below). For directions and more information, call the 24-hour information line at 216-351-6300 (TTY: 216-351-0808) or visit the Metroparks Internet Web site at www.clemetparks.com.

Bedford Reservation, Walton Hills. 🚌 Take RTA 76 bus to corner of Turney and Dunham, then walk south on Dunham for about 2/3 of a mile.

Big Creek Reservation, North entrance, Brooklyn. 🚌 Take RTA 98 bus to main entrance, just east of Tiedeman Road. Or, take RTA 23 bus to Tiedeman and Brookpark, then walk east a few blocks.

Big Creek Reservation, South entrance, Middleburg Heights. 🚌 Take RTA 51X, 251 and 89 buses to Pearl and Fowles, walk west on Fowles to Big Creek Parkway.

Bradley Woods Reservation, Westlake/North Olmsted. 🚌 Take RTA 42, 55SX or 65F to Center Ridge and Crocker, then walk 2/3 of a mile west to Bradley, then south on Bradley. Also, take 75X and 75F buses to Lorain and Barton, then walk 1/3 of a mile west on Barton, then walk north up Bradley.

Brecksville Reservation, Brecksville. 🚌 Served by RTA 77F bus.

Brookside Reservation, Cleveland. 🚌 The RTA 79 buses go to the corner of Park and Fulton, near the park's main entrance. Access from zoo end, via RTA 20, 20A, 20B, 21X, 35, 50, 51X, 807 buses.

Car-Free in Cleveland

Euclid Creek Reservation, Euclid/South Euclid/Richmond Heights. 🚌 Take RTA 34 or 6 buses to Euclid Ave. between Dille and Chardon Rds.

Garfield Park Reservation, Garfield Heights. 🚌 Take RTA 48, 90X or 97X to Broadway and Henry.

Huntington Reservation, Bay Village. 🚌 Served by RTA 31X, 42, 55CF and 55CX buses.

Mill Stream Run Reservation, North entrance, Berea. 🚌 Served by RTA 68, 86 and 89 buses.

Mill Stream Run Reservation, South entrance, Strongsville. 🚌 Take RTA 51X, 89, and 251 buses down Pearl just south of Ohio Turnpike.

North Chagrin Reservation, Mayfield, Gates Mills, Willoughby Hills. 🚌 The RTA 7X and 7F buses stop at the corner of Wilson Mills and SOM Center Rds., which is one mile from the park.

Rocky River Reservation, Detroit Rd. entrance, Rocky River/Lakewood city line. 🚌 Directly served by RTA 55X, 55SX, and 326 buses.

Rocky River Reservation, Puritas entrance, West Park. 🚌 The RTA 78 bus stops at the corner of Grayton and Puritas, just uphill from the park.

Rocky River Reservation, Shepard Lane entrance, North Olmsted. 🚌 Take RTA 53, 75F and 96F buses to the corner of Mastick and Shepard Lane, then walk down the hill to the park.

Rocky River Reservation, Cedar Point/Columbia entrance, North Olmsted. 🚌 Served by RTA 53, 64F and 96F buses.

South Chagrin Reservation, Moreland Hills, Bentleyville. 🚌 The main entrance of this park is a 2.5-mile walk south of RTA 5 bus at Chagrin Blvd. and SOM Center Rd.

Metroparks Zoo, Cleveland. 🚌 Take any of RTA 20 buses or the 21X, 35, or 51X to W. 25th and Broadview. Take the zoo entrance, then walk down a long hill.

GREATER CLEVELAND SPORTS VENUES

Cleveland Browns football, Cleveland Browns Stadium, W. 3rd street and Erieside Ave., Cleveland. ☎440-891-5000. 🚌 Directly served by the W. 3rd Street Rapid station (RTA Blue/67X and Blue 67AX lines) and within a short walk of numerous other regular and special RTA and LAKETRAN buses.

Cleveland Cavaliers basketball, Gund Arena/Gateway, Ontario and Huron Avenues, Cleveland. ☎ 216-420-2200. 🚌 Use Tower City Rapid station (RTA Red/66X/66S, Blue/67X and Green/67AX lines) and walk several

Places to see and things to do

blocks through the enclosed RTA Walkway to Gateway. Also, a majority of regular route RTA bus lines are within a few blocks of Gund Arena, which is also served by special Gateway buses from suburban Park-n-Rides.

Cleveland Crunch soccer, CSU Convocation Center, E. 18th St. and Prospect Ave., Cleveland. ☎ 440-349-2090. 🚌 A majority of RTA, Akron METRO and LAKETRAN bus routes serving downtown are within a few blocks.

Cleveland Indians baseball, Jacobs Field/Gateway, Ontario and Carnegie Avenues, Cleveland. ☎ 216-420-4200. 🚌 Use Tower City Rapid station (RTA Red/66X/66S, Blue/67X and Green/67AX lines) and walk several blocks through the enclosed RTA Walkway to Gateway. Also, a majority of regular route RTA bus lines are within a few blocks of Jacobs Field, which is also served by special RTA and LAKETRAN Gateway buses from suburban Park-n-Rides.

Cleveland Lumberjacks hockey, Gund Arena/Gateway, Ontario and Huron Avenues, Cleveland. ☎ 216-420-0000. 🚌 Use Tower City Rapid station (RTA Red/66X/66S, Blue/67X and Green/67AX lines) and walk several blocks through the enclosed RTA Walkway to Gateway. Also, a majority of regular route RTA bus lines are within a few blocks of Gund Arena, which is also served by special Gateway buses from suburban Park-n-Rides.

Cleveland State Vikings basketball, CSU Convocation Center, E. 18th St. and Prospect Ave., Cleveland. ☎ 216-687-4848. 🚌 A majority of RTA, Akron METRO and LAKETRAN bus routes serving downtown are within a few blocks.

Thistledown Racing Club (thoroughbred horse racing), Warrensville Center and Emery roads, North Randall. ☎ 216-662-8600. 🚌 Take RTA 15, 19, 34 and 41 buses. Note: the 19 and 34 buses terminate at Randall Park Mall, which is immediately south of Thistledown.

Northfield Park Harness racing, 10705 Northfield Rd., Northfield. ☎ 330-467-4101. 🚌 Take RTA 97F to Ford plant and walk 1/2-mile south down Northfield Rd. past the factory. From Akron, take METRO bus 102 (weekdays only). Some trips end at Northfield Plaza, which is 3/4-mile south of the race track.

Car-Free in Cleveland

Greater Cleveland RTA Bus and Rapid routes

This chapter contains key information about the Greater Cleveland RTA's bus and Rapid rail routes: route numbers and names, frequencies of service, starting and ending points, main roads served, earliest and latest service on weekdays, and other important details. The information presented in this chapter is the most recent available as of Fall 1999. Be aware, however, that *routes and service frequencies change* depending upon the season and *RTA is planning some major changes in service* in 2000 that may see some existing routes combined or eliminated and new routes added. We have indicated some of the possible changes in the "Notes" section.

Whatever your travel plans, if you're taking an RTA bus or train route for the first time, it is a good idea to call **RTA's Answerline** at **(216) 621-9500** before you travel. Also, make sure you pick up a copy of the new RTA System Map at any RTA service center or by calling the Answerline to request that one be mailed to you.

Explanation and notes: The information presented is current as of Spring, 1999. Call **RTA's Answerline at (216) 621-9500** for the most up-to-date information. Bus routes are listed in the order found on RTA's Internet Web Site at http://little.nhlink.net/~rta and are not always in numerical order. 1) "M-F peak freq." refers to the frequency of service between 6:00 a.m. and 9:00 a.m. and between 3:00 p.m. and 6:00 p.m. on regular work days. 2) "M-F off-peak freq." refers to service at all other times on regular work days. 3) Service frequency on holidays is the same as Sunday frequency. 4) "Trunk route(s)" refers to the main roads on which a bus route provides service. 5) First and Last buses (or trains) refers to the earliest and latest service provided from the starting point of a route on regular work days. Note that service on Saturdays, Sundays and holidays usually starts later and ends earlier than on regular work days. 6) "N/A" means service Not Available at the indicated time or day.

Rapid transit (rail) routes

Route #	Route name	M-F peak freq.	M-F off-peak freq.	Saturday frequency	Sunday frequency
66X	Airport - Windermere Red Line Rapid	6 to 12	12 to 15	15	15

Start: Cleveland Hopkins Airport. *End:* East Cleveland, Windermere.
First train: 4:32 AM. *Last train:* 9:59 PM.
First train, opposite direction: 3:39 AM. *Last train, opposite direction:* 10:22 PM.
Notes: Some early and late trains do not run east of Tower City. The 66S shuttle bus runs daily between the airport and Tower City from 9:40 PM to 1:10 AM.

67X	Van Aken (Blue / Waterfront Line) Rapid	12	24	30	30

Start: Shaker Heights, Van Aken and Warrensville Center. *End:* Cleveland, South Harbor.
First train: 4:26 AM. *Last train:* 12:55 AM.
First train, opposite direction: 4:02 AM. *Last train, opposite direction:* 12:05 AM.
Notes: Trains do not run on the Waterfront Line portion of the route before 6:00 AM or after 12:05 AM.

67AX	Shaker Blvd. Green Line Rapid	12	24	30	30

Start: Shaker Heights, Shaker and Green. *End:* Cleveland, Tower City.
First train: 5:55 AM. *Last train:* 12:40 AM.
First train, opposite direction: 5:31 AM. *Last train, opposite direction:* 11:50 PM.
Notes:

Greater Cleveland RTA Bus and Rapid Routes

Local, express and flyer bus routes

Route number	Route name	M-F peak freq.	M-F off-peak freq.	Saturday frequency	Sunday frequency
1	**St. Clair**	6-10	10	10-15	30-40
	Start: Euclid, Euclid Square Mall. *End:* Cleveland, Public Square. *Trunk route(s):* St. Clair				
	First bus: 5:10 AM. *Last bus:* 12:45 AM.				
	First bus, opposite direction: 5:19 AM. *Last bus, opposite direction:* 1:10 AM.				
Notes:	Hourly night owl service between St. Clair & E. 152 to Public Square, consult Schedule.				
2	**East 55-East 79**	40	40	45	45
	Start: Cleveland, St. Clair & E. 55. *End:* Cleveland, St. Clair/E. 79. *Trunk route(s):* E. 55, E. 79				
	First bus: 4:50 AM. *Last bus:* 11:18 AM.				
	First bus, opposite direction: 5:55 AM. *Last bus, opposite direction:* 12:25 PM.				
Notes:	Runs one direction on E. 55, loops on Broadway and Union to E. 79, extended service hours on portions of route.				
326	**Detroit - Superior**	5 to 10	10 to 15	15-20	30
	Start: Rocky River, Westgate Transit Center. *End:* Cleveland, E. 129 Loop Park-n-Ride. *Trunk route(s):* Detroit, Superior				
	First bus: 6:00 AM. *Last bus:* 9:47 PM.				
	First bus, opposite direction: 6:12 AM. *Last bus, opposite direction:* 8:05 PM.				
Notes:	Routes runs via Public Square. Hourly night owl service between Rocky River Loop and E. 129/St. Clair. Reduced Sat. service and no Sun. service west of West. Blvd. rapid station.				
3	**Detroit Avenue Shuttle**	30	30	30	30
	Start: Cleveland, West 65th and Detroit. *End:* Cleveland, West 65th and Detroit (Loop Route). *Trunk route(s):* Detroit				
	First bus: 5:30 AM. *Last bus:* 9:30 AM.				
	First bus, opposite direction: 7:30 AM. *Last bus, opposite direction:* 12:00 AM.				
Notes:	Morning and evening service only Mon-Sat. Sunday service all day. Provides access via pedestrian walkway to West Blvd./Cudell Red Line Rapid station.				
4	**Payne - Wade Park**	25	40-60	40 - 60	75
	Start: Cleveland, Superior Rapid Station. *End:* Cleveland, Public Square. *Trunk route(s):* Wade Park, Payne				
	First bus: 5:41 AM. *Last bus:* 12:41 AM.				
	First bus, opposite direction: 5:04 AM. *Last bus, opposite direction:* 12:12 AM.				
Notes:					
5	**Chagrin Blvd.**	20	30	30	30
	Start: Chagrin Falls. *End:* Shaker Heights, Van Aken Rapid Station. *Trunk route(s):* Chagrin Blvd.				
	First bus: 5:25 AM. *Last bus:* 11:45 PM.				
	First bus, opposite direction: 5:51 AM. *Last bus, opposite direction:* 11:58 PM.				
Notes:	No service east of Lander Blvd. after 8:45 PM M-F and after 7:00 PM Sat & Sun.				
6	**Euclid Ave.**	6	7-15	10	20
	Start: Euclid, E. 276 & Tungsten. *End:* Cleveland, Public Square. *Trunk route(s):* Euclid Ave.				
	First bus: 12:40 AM. *Last bus:* 12:25 AM.				
	First bus, opposite direction: 12:09 AM. *Last bus, opposite direction:* 11:39 PM.				
Notes:	Night owl service between midnight and 5:30 AM runs every 20 to 30 minutes.				
7F	**Monticello - Euclid Hts.**	15-20	N/A	N/A	N/A
	Start: Gates Mills, Tower Lane. *End:* Cleveland, Public Square. *Trunk route(s):* Wilson Mills, Monticello, Euclid Heights Blvd.				
	First bus: 4:40 PM. *Last bus:* 5:50 PM.				
	First bus, opposite direction: 6:10 AM. *Last bus, opposite direction:* 7:30 AM.				
Notes:	7F runs during weekday rush hours only, using the same route as the 7X but continuing to Public Square along Euclid Ave.				

Car-Free in Cleveland

Route number	Route name	M-F peak freq.	M-F off-peak freq.	Saturday frequency	Sunday frequency
7X	**Monticello - Euclid Hts.**	15-30	40	60	60
	Start: Gates Mills, Tower Lane. *End:* University Circle Rapid Station. *Trunk route(s):* Wilson Mills, Monticello, Euclid Heights Blvd.				
	First bus: 5:03 AM. *Last bus:* 9:55 PM.				
	First bus, opposite direction: 5:50 AM. *Last bus, opposite direction:* 7:20 PM.				
Notes:	Buses before 5:50 AM and after 7:20 PM depart from Richmond Mall, Mayfield Hts.				
8	**Cedar Ave.**	25-30	35	30-60	60
	Start: Cleveland, University Circle Rapid Station. *End:* Cleveland, Public Square. *Trunk route(s):* Cedar Ave., Prospect				
	First bus: 5:33 AM. *Last bus:* 12:33 AM.				
	First bus, opposite direction: 5:09 AM. *Last bus, opposite direction:* 12:11 AM.				
Notes:	Weekdays from 6:00 AM to 6:00 PM, the route includes a downtown loop run. Eastbound Service originates at St. Clair/Mall				
9X	**Mayfield**	20-50	20	30-45	40-50
	Start: Gates Mills, Tower Lane. *End:* Cleveland, Public Square. *Trunk route(s):* Mayfield, Euclid				
	First bus: 4:45 AM. *Last bus:* 12:50 AM.				
	First bus, opposite direction: 5:25 AM. *Last bus, opposite direction:* 11:56 PM.				
Notes:	Four trips in morning originate at Ridgebury Blvd. and SOM Center and four trips in afternoon end there. Some 9X buses stop at Severance Center on Mayfield Rd. in Cleveland Heights. Also see the 9F bus which covers fewer stops on the same route.				
9BX	**Mayfield**	15	50	30-45	N/A
	Start: Mayfield Heights, Richmond Mall. *End:* Cleveland, Public Square. *Trunk route(s):* Mayfield, Euclid				
	First bus: 7:20 AM. *Last bus:* 6:10 PM.				
	First bus, opposite direction: 6:29 AM. *Last bus, opposite direction:* 5:55 PM.				
Notes:	9BX serves same route as 9X and 9F west of Richmond Rd. in Mayfield Heights. Some buses serve the Windermere Rapid station. Consult schedule for details.				
9F	**Mayfield**	10-20	N/A	N/A	N/A
	Start: Gates Mills, Tower Lane. *End:* Cleveland, Public Square. *Trunk route(s):* Mayfield, Euclid				
	First bus: 4:00 AM. *Last bus:* 6:00 PM.				
	First bus, opposite direction: 5:55 AM. *Last bus, opposite direction:* 7:50 AM.				
Notes:	Weekday rush-hour service only. Morning service between 5:45 AM and 7:50 AM in westbound direction only. Afternoon service between 4:00 PM and 6:00 PM in eastbound direction only.				
10	**East 105**	7	10 to 20	20	20
	Start: Cleveland, Turney & Ella. *End:* Cleveland, Dupont near St. Clair & E. 105. *Trunk route(s):* E. 93, Woodhill, E. 105				
	First bus: 5:16 AM. *Last bus:* 11:41 PM.				
	First bus, opposite direction: 4:38 AM. *Last bus, opposite direction:* 12:30 AM.				
Notes:	Night hour service originates from Harvard Garage at Harvard & E. 74. Some evening buses continue south to Marymount Hospital on McCracken. Consult RTA Answerline.				
14	**Kinsman**	10	10	15	25
	Start: Shaker Heights, Van Aken Rapid Station. *End:* Cleveland, Public Square. *Trunk route(s):* Harvard, Chagrin, Kinsman				
	First bus: 1:10 AM. *Last bus:* 12:40 AM.				
	First bus, opposite direction: 12:20 AM. *Last bus, opposite direction:* 11:47 PM.				
Notes:	Some buses continue to Metro Health Center. Weekday work hour service includes a downtown loop. Night owl service.				
15	**Union**	10 to 15	30	15-30	30-35
	Start: North Randall, Randall Park Mall. *End:* Cleveland, Public Square. *Trunk route(s):* Union, Harvard				
	First bus: 5:10 AM. *Last bus:* 1:10 AM.				
	First bus, opposite direction: 4:05 AM. *Last bus, opposite direction:* 12:04 PM.				
Notes:	From 6:10 am to 6:25 pm, Buses departing Downtown leave from West Prospect. Other times, Departures from West Roadway/Superior				

Greater Cleveland RTA Bus and Rapid Routes

Route number	Route name	M-F peak freq.	M-F off-peak freq.	Saturday frequency	Sunday frequency
15A	Union - Walden	30	N/A	N/A	N/A

Notes: *Start:* North Randall, Randall Park Mall. *End:* Cleveland, Public Square. *Trunk route(s):* Union, Walden
First bus: 4:05 PM. *Last bus:* 5:35 PM.
First bus, opposite direction: 5:59 AM. *Last bus, opposite direction:* 7:24 AM.
Rush hour service only on weekdays. Same route as 15 except for 46-block distance between E. 176 and E. 131. Westbound service 5:59 AM to 7:24 AM; eastbound service 4:05 PM to 5:35 PM.

15F	Warrensville Heights Flyer	30	N/A	N/A	N/A

Notes: *Start:* Warrensville Heights, Country Lane near Emery and Richmond. *End:* Cleveland, West Prospect. *Trunk route(s):* I 480 and I-77
First bus: 3:32 PM. *Last bus:* 6:32 PM.
First bus, opposite direction: 4:57 AM. *Last bus, opposite direction:* 7:57 AM.
Commuter buses with westbound service in the morning and eastbound service in the afternoon.

16	East 55	25	25-50	20	20

Notes: *Start:* Cleveland, Harvard Rd. RTA Garage. *End:* Cleveland, E 55 and Woodland. *Trunk route(s):* E. 55, Washington Park
First bus: 3:41 AM. *Last bus:* 12:45 AM.
First bus, opposite direction: 3:58 AM. *Last bus, opposite direction:* 1:05 AM.
About half of #16 buses run a bit farther west to the LTV Loop. Not officially a "night owl" bus, but service available all day except between 12:45 a.m. and 3:41 a.m.

19	Broadway - Miles	12	30	30	30

Notes: *Start:* North Randall, Randall Park Mall. *End:* Cleveland, Public Square. *Trunk route(s):* Miles, Broadway
First bus: 1:09 AM. *Last bus:* 11:53 PM.
First bus, opposite direction: 1:40 AM. *Last bus, opposite direction:* 12:40 AM.
Night owl service runs between Miles & E. 131 and Public Square only. See information for the 19S Miles Shuttle for connections to Commerce Park.

19S	Miles Shuttle	40-60	N/A	N/A	N/A

Notes: *Start:* North Randall, Randall Park Mall. *End:* Warrensville Heights, Commerce Park Blvd. *Trunk route(s):* Miles
First bus: 5:50 AM. *Last bus:* 5:45 PM.
First bus, opposite direction: 5:31 AM. *Last bus, opposite direction:* 5:25 AM.
Commute hour service only between Commerce Park and Randall Park Mall.

20	West 11 - Broadview	30	N/A	N/A	N/A

Notes: *Start:* Cleveland, West 33 Loop near Brookpark and Broadview. *End:* Cleveland, St Clair and East 12. *Trunk route(s):* West 25, Broadview
First bus: 6:43 AM. *Last bus:* 7:48 AM.
First bus, opposite direction: 4:10 PM. *Last bus, opposite direction:* 5:40 PM.
Three northbound morning and four southbound afternoon buses weekdays.

20A	West 25 - State	15-20	60	35-50	60

Notes: *Start:* Parma, State and Sprague. *End:* Cleveland, Public Square. *Trunk route(s):* West 25, State
First bus: 7:22 AM. *Last bus:* 11:54 PM.
First bus, opposite direction: 5:40 AM. *Last bus, opposite direction:* 12:38 AM.
Additional service availaible to and from Parmatown, Pleasant Valley Shopping Ctr., Royalton/Bennett. Consult RTA Answerline. Night owl service provided between Brookpark & West 33rd to Public Square.

21X	West 25 - State	15	N/A	N/A	N/A

Notes: *Start:* North Royalton, Bennett and Royalton. *End:* Cleveland, Public Square. *Trunk route(s):* West 25, State
First bus: 5:25 AM. *Last bus:* 7:59 AM.
First bus, opposite direction: 3:45 PM. *Last bus, opposite direction:* 6:03 PM.
Service extends until 12:35 AM to Superior/East Roadway and through the evening once an hour

Car-Free in Cleveland

Route number	Route name	M-F peak freq.	M-F off-peak freq.	Saturday frequency	Sunday frequency
20B	**West 25 - Pearl**	10	45	35-45	60

Start: Parma, Parmatown Mall. *End:* Cleveland, Public Square. *Trunk route(s):* West 25, Pearl
First bus: 5:38 AM. *Last bus:* 11:42 PM.
First bus, opposite direction: 6:27 AM. *Last bus, opposite direction:* 10:55 PM.
Notes: Service extends to Superior/East Roadway until 12:24 AM

22	**Lorain Avenue**	10	20	15-30	30

Start: Fairview Park, Westgate Transit Center. *End:* Cleveland, East 12-Rockwell. *Trunk route(s):* Lorain, Superior
First bus: 1:10 AM. *Last bus:* 12:10 AM.
First bus, opposite direction: 12:33 AM. *Last bus, opposite direction:* 11:30 PM.
Notes: Night owl service available between Fairview Hospital and Public Square, but note that between 1:00 AM and 3:00 AM buses arrive/leave Cleveland Hopkins Airport. RTA proposes some routing changes to this route in the Spring of 2000.

23	**Clark - Ridge**	30	60	60	60

Start: Parma, Parmatown. *End:* Cleveland, East 12-Rockwell. *Trunk route(s):* Clark, Ridge
First bus: 6:02 AM. *Last bus:* 9:58 PM.
First bus, opposite direction: 6:30 AM. *Last bus, opposite direction:* 6:00 PM.
Notes: Service extends until 12:25 at Superior East Roadway only. Service is available at some stops as early as 4: am. Route zigzags - see map, call Answerline

25B	**Madison - Buckeye**	15-20	30	60	60

Start: Fairview Park, Westgate Transit Center. *End:* Cleveland, Shaker Square. *Trunk route(s):* Madison, Buckeye
First bus: 6:30 AM. *Last bus:* 10:00 PM.
First bus, opposite direction: 5:10 AM. *Last bus, opposite direction:* 1:00 AM.
Notes: Service Begins at 4:30 a.m. at Madison & Cordova; last bus returns there at 1:54 a.m. This route runs via Public Square and has several connections to Red, Blue and Green Rapid lines.

25W	**Madison - Woodland**	15-20	30	60	60

Start: Fairview Park, Westgate Transit Center. *End:* Cleveland, Shaker Square. *Trunk route(s):* Maison, Woodland
First bus: 6:30 AM. *Last bus:* 11:36 PM.
First bus, opposite direction: 5:10 AM. *Last bus, opposite direction:* 1:00 AM.
Notes: Service Begins at 4:30 a.m. at Madison & Cordova; last bus returns there at 1:54 a.m. This route runs via Public Square and has several connections to Red, Blue and Green Rapid lines.

30	**East 140 - Hayden**	20	30-35	30	60

Start: Euclid, East 185 and Lake Shore. *End:* East Cleveland, Windermere Rapid Station. *Trunk route(s):* East 140, Lake Shore
First bus: 5:05 AM. *Last bus:* 12:40 AM.
First bus, opposite direction: 4:28 AM. *Last bus, opposite direction:* 1:01 AM.
Notes: Route ends near Merida Euclid Hospital; not all buses lift equipped

31X	**Avon Lake**	20-60	N/A	N/A	N/A

Start: Avon Lake, Lake and Moore. *End:* Cleveland, East 17th and Euclid. *Trunk route(s):* West Shoreway, Clifton
First bus: 4:40 PM. *Last bus:* 6:10 PM.
First bus, opposite direction: 6:25 AM. *Last bus, opposite direction:* 7:30 AM.
Notes: Westbound route begins at East 17 and Payne and ends at Miller and Lake in Avon Lake. Commuter service, 4 runs each direction. No Saturday, Sunday or holiday service. RTA proposes rerouting to I-90 and slightly changing departure times in the Fall of 1999

32CX	**Cedar**	15-30	45-50	20-30	20-30

Start: Gates Mills, Gilmour Academy. *End:* Cleveland, Public Square. *Trunk route(s):* Cedar, Carnegie
First bus: 4:45 AM. *Last bus:* 11:57 PM.
First bus, opposite direction: 6:00 AM. *Last bus, opposite direction:* 11:33 PM.
Notes: Service continues from University Circle to downtown Cleveland during weekday rush hours only (takes an additional 22 minutes).

Greater Cleveland RTA Bus and Rapid Routes

Route number	Route name	M-F peak freq.	M-F off-peak freq.	Saturday frequency	Sunday frequency
32SX	Cedar - Silsby	20	20	N/A	N/A
	Start: Gates Mills, Gilmour Academy. *End:* Cleveland, Public Square. *Trunk route(s):* Cedar, Carnegie *First bus:* 5:10 AM. *Last bus:* 5:19 PM. *First bus, opposite direction:* 6:16 AM. *Last bus, opposite direction:* 4:57 PM.				
Notes:	Service frequency increases between Cedar/Menorah Park and University Circle. No Evening/Sat./Sun./holiday service. Service continues from University Circle to downtown Cleveland during weekday rush hours only (takes an additional 22 minutes).				
32WX	Cedar - Washington	15-40	30-60	N/A	N/A
	Start: University Heights, Washington and Belvior. *End:* Cleveland, Public Square. *Trunk route(s):* Cedar, Carnegie *First bus:* 6:17 AM. *Last bus:* 6:44 PM. *First bus, opposite direction:* 6:38 AM. *Last bus, opposite direction:* 7:03 PM.				
Notes:	Access to John Carroll University. Service continues from University Circle to downtown Cleveland during weekday rush hours only.				
33	Central	20-30	60	50	N/A
	Start: Cleveland, Central and East 83. *End:* St. Clair/Mall. *Trunk route(s):* Central, Prospect *First bus:* 6:27 AM. *Last bus:* 6:27 PM. *First bus, opposite direction:* 5:53 AM. *Last bus, opposite direction:* 5:50 PM.				
Notes:	No Sunday/holiday Service				
34	East 200 - Green	25	45	65	65
	Start: Euclid, E. 185 and Lake Shore. *End:* Randall Park Mall. *Trunk route(s):* E. 200, Green *First bus:* 6:17 AM. *Last bus:* 9:50 PM. *First bus, opposite direction:* 5:44 AM. *Last bus, opposite direction:* 10:50 PM.				
Notes:	Connects with Green Line Light Rail				
35	Broadview - Quincy	20	20-40	20-40	60
	Start: North Royalton, York-North Royalton Service Yard. *End:* Cleveland, St. Luke's Hospital. *Trunk route(s):* Broadview, West 25, Quincy *First bus:* 5:00 AM. *Last bus:* 6:01 PM. *First bus, opposite direction:* 5:05 AM. *Last bus, opposite direction:* 11:35 PM.				
Notes:	Route via Public Square. Some reverse commute service is limited to weekdays. Sat./Sun./holiday service starts/ends at Broadview Center.				
35F	Broadview - Pleasant Valley	10	N/A	N/A	N/A
	Start: Parma, Broadview and Pleasant Valley. *End:* Cleveland, Public Square. *Trunk route(s):* I-77, I-480 *First bus:* 6:54 AM. *Last bus:* 7:46 AM. *First bus, opposite direction:* 4:26 PM. *Last bus, opposite direction:* 5:16 PM.				
Notes:	Travels via Broadview, Brookpark, I-77 and I-480. Southbound trips begin at Cleveland State University (East 22nd and Euclid).				
135	Broadview - North Royalton	10	N/A	N/A	N/A
	Start: North Royalton, York-North Royalton Service Yard. *End:* Cleveland, Public Square. *Trunk route(s):* I-77 *First bus:* 6:14 AM. *Last bus:* 7:32 AM. *First bus, opposite direction:* 4:25 PM. *Last bus, opposite direction:* 5:20 PM.				
Notes:	Route via Pleasant Valley Rd. and I-77 to Broadview.				
36	Eddy	45	45	45	45
	Start: Superior Rapid Station. *End:* Coit/Kirby. *Trunk route(s):* Eddy *First bus:* 5:38 AM. *Last bus:* 10:26 PM. *First bus, opposite direction:* 5:51 AM. *Last bus, opposite direction:* 10:39 PM.				
Notes:	All buses are lift equipped; connects with Red Line Rail; stops at Merida Huron Hospital				
37	East 185 - Taylor	30-45	30-60	60	70
	Start: Euclid, East 185 and Lake Shore. *End:* Shaker Hts., Lee & Parkland. *Trunk route(s):* East 185, East 152, Taylor *First bus:* 5:04 AM. *Last bus:* 9:04 PM. *First bus, opposite direction:* 5:10 AM. *Last bus, opposite direction:* 10:25 PM.				
Notes:	Some weekday trips do go to Windermere Rapid. First 2 northbound and last 2 southbound buses serve Windermere to Shaker Rapid only. Also serves Meridia Euclid Hospital.				

Car-Free in Cleveland

Route number	Route name	M-F peak freq.	M-F off-peak freq.	Saturday frequency	Sunday frequency
38	**Payne-Hough**	30	40-60	40-60	75
	Start: Cleveland, University Circle Rapid Station. *End:* Cleveland, Public Square. *Trunk route(s):* Hough, Payne *First bus:* 5:55 AM. *Last bus:* 11:56 PM. *First bus, opposite direction:* 5:21 AM. *Last bus, opposite direction:* 11:08 PM.				
Notes:					
39X	**Lake Shore Blvd.**	30-70	60	40-90	120
	Start: Willowick, Shoregate Shopping Center. *End:* Cleveland, Public Square. *Trunk route(s):* Lakeshore, I-90 *First bus:* 6:40 AM. *Last bus:* 12:28 AM. *First bus, opposite direction:* 5:23 AM. *Last bus, opposite direction:* 12:19 AM.				
Notes:	The 39X route runs on I-90 around Bratenahl while the 39BX serves it on Lake Shore Blvd. The two routes rejoin at East 140th Street. Not all buses operate out to Willowick/Shoregate Shopping Center. Fare to Wickliffe is $2.50.				
39BX	**Lake Shore Blvd.**	15-30	60	80	120
	Start: Willowick, Shoregate Shopping Center. *End:* Cleveland, Public Square. *Trunk route(s):* Lakeshore, I-90 *First bus:* 5:50 AM. *Last bus:* 9:05 PM. *First bus, opposite direction:* 5:42 AM. *Last bus, opposite direction:* 5:37 PM.				
Notes:	Most Ebound service from E.3/Rockwell. The 39BX route serves Bratenahl while the 39X bypasses it on I-90. They rejoin at E.140th Street. Not all buses operate out to Willowick/Shoregate Center. Fare to Wickliffe is $2.50. Connect to LAKETRAN at Shoregate.				
39F	**Lake Shore Blvd.**	12 to 20	N/A	N/A	N/A
	Start: Willowick, Shoregate Shopping Center. *End:* Cleveland, East 3 and Rockwell. *Trunk route(s):* Lakeshore, I-90 *First bus:* 3:15 PM. *Last bus:* 6:30 PM. *First bus, opposite direction:* 6:07 AM. *Last bus, opposite direction:* 8:05 AM.				
Notes:	Commuter service. The 39F route splits east of East 222nd Street--one to Willowick / Shoregate Shopping Center and the other to the Euclid Park & Ride. Fare to Wickliffe is $2.50. Connect to LAKETRAN buses at Shoregate.				
40	**Lakeview - Lee**	15	30	30	40
	Start: Bratenahl/Cleveland, Eddy & Hazeldell. *End:* Maple Hts., Southgate USA. *Trunk route(s):* Lakeview, Superior, Lee *First bus:* 4:06 AM. *Last bus:* 12:28 AM. *First bus, opposite direction:* 4:50 AM. *Last bus, opposite direction:* 1:35 AM.				
Notes:	Some early and late buses only go as far north as Mayfield and Lee.				
41A	**Warrensville - Aurora**	50	50	50	N/A
	Start: East Cleveland, Windermere Rapid station , Solon, Cochran Rd./Glen Willow , Noble/Warrensville/Libby/Aurora. *End:* Solon Square Shopping Ctr.. *Trunk route(s):* Aurora, Warrensville *First bus:* 5:27 AM. *Last bus:* 10:56 PM. *First bus, opposite direction:* 4:26 AM. *Last bus, opposite direction:* 9:35 PM.				
Notes:	Some buses end their routes at different major employers in Bedford Hts., Solon, and Glen Willow. For Sunday/Holiday service, see the 41C route.				
41C	**Warrensville - Columbus**	40	60	60	50
	Start: East Cleveland, Windermere Rapid station. *End:* Solon, Solon Square Shopping Center. *Trunk route(s):* Aurora, Northfield, Warrensville *First bus:* 5:35 AM. *Last bus:* 11:35 PM. *First bus, opposite direction:* 4:10 AM. *Last bus, opposite direction:* 10:00 PM.				
Notes:	Some buses operate via Kimberly and Eldridge in Bedford Hts.				
41S	**Noble-Taylor**	N/A	40-50	50-60	N/A
	Start: East Cleveland, Windermere Rapid station. *End:* Cleveland Hts, Severance Shopping Center. *Trunk route(s):* Taylor, Noble *First bus:* 6:55 PM. *Last bus:* 10:17 PM. *First bus, opposite direction:* N/A. *Last bus, opposite direction:* N/A.				
Notes:	Loop-shaped routes operates during evenings of weekdays and Saturdays only. See the 9X, 9BX, 37, 41A, 41C buses for additional service.				

Greater Cleveland RTA Bus and Rapid Routes

Route number	Route name	M-F peak freq.	M-F off-peak freq.	Saturday frequency	Sunday frequency
44	Snow - Rockside	20-90	120	N/A	N/A

Start: Brook Park, Brookpark Rapid station. *End:* Garfield Hts., Garfield Mall at Turney. *Trunk route(s):* Henry Ford Blvd., Snow, Rockside
First bus: 7:26 AM. *Last bus:* 5:20 PM.
First bus, opposite direction: 6:37 AM. *Last bus, opposite direction:* 6:13 PM.
Notes: First eastbound bus originates at Snow and Ridge Roads in Parma at 6:06 AM.

45	West 65 - Ridge	100	100	90	90

Start: Lakewood/Cleveland, Clifton & West 115. *End:* Parma, Parmatown Mall. *Trunk route(s):* Clifton, Detroit, West 65th, Ridge
First bus: 6:15 AM. *Last bus:* 9:45 PM.
First bus, opposite direction: 7:05 AM. *Last bus, opposite direction:* 10:30 PM.
Notes:

46	Detroit Road - Delaware	15-35	N/A	N/A	N/A

Start: Westlake, Lorain County line & Detroit. *End:* Cleveland, Triskett Red Line Rapid Station. *Trunk route(s):* Detroit, Hilliard, Lakewood Hts. Blvd.
First bus: 5:38 PM. *Last bus:* 6:37 PM.
First bus, opposite direction: 5:16 AM. *Last bus, opposite direction:* 6:48 AM.
Notes: Buses operate in rush hours only, for reverse commuters who live in the city and work in the suburbs. RTA may extend service to and from downtown Cleveland in the Fall of 1999.

46F	Westlake	15-30	N/A	N/A	N/A

Start: Westlake, Lorain County line & Detroit. *End:* Cleveland, Chester & East 18th. *Trunk route(s):* Detroit, Clifton, West Shoreway
First bus: 6:04 AM. *Last bus:* 7:50 AM.
First bus, opposite direction: 4:38 PM. *Last bus, opposite direction:* 5:58 PM.
Notes: 6 commute and 3 reverse-commute buses operate in rush hours to and from Public Sq.

48	University Circle-East 131	20	40-60	70	90

Start: Maple Hts., Marymount Hospital & McCracken. *End:* Cleveland, Euclid & East 93. *Trunk route(s):* Adelbert, Fairhill, Shaker Square, East 131
First bus: 5:36 AM. *Last bus:* 1:14 AM.
First bus, opposite direction: 5:25 AM. *Last bus, opposite direction:* 12:30 AM.
Notes: More frequent service is available north of Miles & East 131st, where the 48 route is combined with the 48A, making service twice as frequent.

48A	University Circle-East 131	20	40-60	70	90

Start: Cleveland, South Miles & East 177. *End:* Cleveland, Euclid & East 93. *Trunk route(s):* Adelbert, Fairhill, Shaker Square, East 131
First bus: 4:19 AM. *Last bus:* 1:40 AM.
First bus, opposite direction: 5:05 AM. *Last bus, opposite direction:* 1:00 AM.
Notes: More frequent service is available north of Miles & East 131st, where the 48A route is combined with the 48, making service twice as frequent.

50	East 116/Harvard/Memphis	20	30	30	40

Start: Cleveland, Veteran's Hospital East. *End:* Lakewood, West 117 & Clifton. *Trunk route(s):* M.L. King, Harvard-Denison, Memphis, West 117th
First bus: 5:05 AM. *Last bus:* 10:40 PM.
First bus, opposite direction: 5:04 AM. *Last bus, opposite direction:* 9:50 PM.
Notes: Route operates around the west, south and east sides of the city. Some rush-hour trips run through the American Greetings plant in Brooklyn.

51X	West 25th - Pearl	10 to 30	40	45	45

Start: Strongsville, Drake and Howe near South Park Mall OR Strongsville Park-n-Ride lot. *End:* Cleveland State University (East 22nd and Chester). *Trunk route(s):* Pearl Rd., West 25th
First bus: 5:19 AM. *Last bus:* 10:27 PM.
First bus, opposite direction: 5:46 AM. *Last bus, opposite direction:* 10:10 PM.
Notes: Most rush hour buses depart from and terminate at the Strongsville Park-n-Ride lot. Others depart from Pearl and West 130.

Car-Free in Cleveland

Route number	Route name	M-F peak freq.	M-F off-peak freq.	Saturday frequency	Sunday frequency
51F	I-71/Pearl Rd. Flyer (Drake - Howard)	14-35	N/A	N/A	N/A

Start: Strongsville, Drake and Howe near South Park Mall. *End:* Cleveland State University (East 22nd and Chester). *Trunk route(s):* I-71
First bus: 6:15 AM. *Last bus:* 7:55 AM.
First bus, opposite direction: 4:10 PM. *Last bus, opposite direction:* 5:31 PM.
Notes: Morning service only northbound and afternoon service only southbound.

	Great Northern - Center Ridge	60	60	60	N/A
53					

Start: North Olmsted, Great Northern Plaza. *End:* West 210 and Center Ridge Rd..
Trunk route(s): Country Club, Center Ridge
First bus: 10:15 AM. *Last bus:* 6:15 PM.
First bus, opposite direction: 9:15 AM. *Last bus, opposite direction:* 5:15 PM.
Notes: RTA #53 is a loop route beginning and ending at Great Northern Plaza with the farthest station from the origin at W. 210 and Center Ridge. RTA proposes modifications in this route starting in the Spring of 2000.

	Clifton	10-20	60	60	60
55X					

Start: Westlake, Lorain County Line on Detroit or Rocky River Loop on Detroit near Sloane. *End:* Cleveland, E. 21 & Euclid. *Trunk routes:* Clifton, W. Shoreway
First bus: 5:07 AM. *Last bus:* 12:10 AM.
First bus, opposite direction: 6:42 AM. *Last bus, opposite direction:* 12:40 AM.
Notes: Sat service provides only 2 eastbound and 4 westbound buses between 8:28 PM and 11:13 PM. Sun service provides 6 buses in each direction between 6:40 AM and 9:40 AM and 7:10 PM and 9:10 PM.

	Clifton - Gold Coast	20-30	35-45	N/A	N/A
55AX					

Start: Lakewood, Lakewood Park at Belle and Clifton. *End:* Cleveland, East 21 and Euclid. *Trunk route(s):* Clifton, West Shoreway, Lakeside
First bus: 6:27 AM. *Last bus:* 5:13 PM.
First bus, opposite direction: 6:58 AM. *Last bus, opposite direction:* 6:05 PM.
Notes: RTA proposes eliminating this route but modifying the 55NX to serve its routing in Fall 1999.

	Clifton - Lake	30	60	60	N/A
55CX					

Start: Bay Village, Cahoon Park at Cahoon and Wolf. *End:* Cleveland, East 21 and Euclid. *Trunk route(s):* Clifton, West Shoreway, Lakeside
First bus: 8:04 AM. *Last bus:* 10:51 PM.
First bus, opposite direction: 7:09 AM. *Last bus, opposite direction:* 10:10 PM.
Notes: Eastbound buses after 6:30 PM terminate at Clifton and West 130; Westbound buses before 7:09 AM begin at Clifton and West 130.

	Clifton - Lake	9-26	N/A	N/A	N/A
55CF					

Start: Bay Village, Cahoon Park at Cahoon and Wolf. *End:* Cleveland, East 21 and Euclid. *Trunk route(s):* Clifton, West Shoreway, Lakeside
First bus: 5:47 AM. *Last bus:* 7:46 AM.
First bus, opposite direction: 4:09 PM. *Last bus, opposite direction:* 5:50 PM.
Notes: Flyer service during morning hours (eastbound) and afternoon hours (westbound) only. RTA proposes rerouting this bus to use I-90 starting in the Fall of 1999.

	Clifton - Wagar	15	45-60	60	120
55NX					

Start: Rocky River, Wooster and Center Ridge. *End:* Cleveland, East 21 and Euclid. *Trunk route(s):* Clifton, West Shoreway, Lakeside
First bus: 6:23 AM. *Last bus:* 8:13 PM.
First bus, opposite direction: 7:10 AM. *Last bus, opposite direction:* 8:20 PM.
Notes: Some buses terminate at Public Square and do not continue to E. 21 and Euclid. This bus shares much of the 55SX route.

	Clifton - Wooster	12-20	60	45-60	120
55SX					

Start: Westlake, Westlake Health Campus. *End:* Cleveland, East 21 and Euclid or Public Square. *Trunk route(s):* Center Ridge, Clifton, West Shoreway, Lakeside
First bus: 6:12 AM. *Last bus:* 10:10 PM.
First bus, opposite direction: 5:42 AM. *Last bus, opposite direction:* 9:00 PM.
Notes: Some buses terminate at Public Square and do not continue to E. 21 and Euclid. This bus shares much of the 55NX route.

Greater Cleveland RTA Bus and Rapid Routes

Route number	Route name	M-F peak freq.	M-F off-peak freq.	Saturday frequency	Sunday frequency
63F	**Great Northern Park n Ride Flyer**	30	N/A	N/A	N/A
	Start: North Olmsted, Lorain County Line. *End:* Cleveland, E. 21st and Euclid. *Trunk route(s):* Lorain, Christmant, McKenzie, Brookpark, I-71				
	First bus: 6:04 AM. *Last bus:* 7:06 AM.				
	First bus, opposite direction: 4:10 PM. *Last bus, opposite direction:* 5:30 PM.				
Notes:	Connects with Lorain Co. Transit at 7:06 a.m. and 5:30 p.m. at Lorain Co. Line. One morning Westbound trip to Lorain-Dover Ctr. leaves E. 21st/Euclid at 7:50 am.				
64F	**Olmsted Falls**	20 to 30	N/A	N/A	N/A
	Start: North Olmsted, Butternut Ridge and Great Northern. *End:* Cleveland, East 21 and Euclid. *Trunk route(s):* I-480, I-71				
	First bus: 6:27 AM. *Last bus:* 7:20 AM.				
	First bus, opposite direction: 4:35 PM. *Last bus, opposite direction:* 5:25 PM.				
Notes:	Only three eastbound morning buses and three westbound afternoon buses.				
65F	**Hilliard**	30	N/A	N/A	N/A
	Start: Westlake, Westlake Health Campus near Center Ridge and Crocker. *End:* Cleveland, East 17 and Euclid. *Trunk route(s):* I-90				
	First bus: 6:31 AM. *Last bus:* 7:31 AM.				
	First bus, opposite direction: 4:34 PM. *Last bus, opposite direction:* 5:34 PM.				
Notes:	Only three morning eastbound buses and three afternoon westbound buses. RTA proposes changes to this route in the Fall of 1999.				
68	**Bagley - Grantwood**	60	60	90	N/A
	Start: Parma, Brookpark and West 33rd. *End:* North Olmsted, Great Northern Park-n-Ride. *Trunk route(s):* Bagley, Ridgewood				
	First bus: 5:31 AM. *Last bus:* 6:05 PM.				
	First bus, opposite direction: 6:35 AM. *Last bus, opposite direction:* 7:30 PM.				
Notes:	A circuitous route through southwest suburbs that includes stops at Parmatown, Southland Shopping Center, Baldwin Wallace College and Town & Country Plaza.				
70	**Bunts - West 150**	40	40 to 60	60	60
	Start: Middleburg Heights, Southland Shopping Center at Pearl and W. 130th. *End:* Lakewood, Lakewood Park at Lake and Belle. *Trunk route(s):* W. 150th, W. 140th, Bunts				
	First bus: 5:40 AM. *Last bus:* 10:50 PM.				
	First bus, opposite direction: 5:00 AM. *Last bus, opposite direction:* 9:40 PM.				
Notes:	A north-south west side route with stops at W. 150th/Puritas and Triskett Red Line Rapid stations. Some early and late buses do not serve all stops.				
75X	**North Olmsted**	10 to 15	30-60	30-45	40-60
	Start: North Olmsted, Lorain County Line. *End:* Cleveland, East 21st and Euclid. *Trunk route(s):* Lorain, W.117, and West Shoreway				
	First bus: 4:25 AM. *Last bus:* 12:18 AM.				
	First bus, opposite direction: 5:25 AM. *Last bus, opposite direction:* 1:20 AM.				
Notes:	Connects with Lorain County Transit five times per day in each direction. Weekend service only to W.117 and Madison and not to downtown Cleveland. One rush hour bus each direction also serves Porter, Oring, Lansing, Devon, Tudor, and Berkshire roads.				
75F	**North Olmsted**	30	N/A	N/A	N/A
	Start: North Olmsted, Lorain County Line. *End:* Cleveland, East 21st and Euclid. *Trunk route(s):* Lorain, W.220, Brookpark, I-71				
	First bus: 4:30 PM. *Last bus:* 5:36 PM.				
	First bus, opposite direction: 6:22 AM. *Last bus, opposite direction:* 7:12 AM.				
Notes:	Three morning eastbound buses and three afternoon westbound buses. Serves Great Northern Mall.				
76X	**Broadway - Turney**	25-45	60	60	N/A
	Start: Maple Heights, Southgate USA Shopping Center at Libby and Warrensville Center Rd.. *End:* Cleveland, Public Square or E. 13 and Payne. *Trunk route(s):* Turney, Broadway				
	First bus: 4:57 AM. *Last bus:* 10:30 PM.				
	First bus, opposite direction: 5:58 AM. *Last bus, opposite direction:* 11:28 PM.				
Notes:	Northbound buses after 7:22 PM originate from Broadway and Warrensville Center and southbound buses after 6:40 PM terminate there.				

Car-Free in Cleveland

Route number	Route name	M-F peak freq.	M-F off-peak freq.	Saturday frequency	Sunday frequency
76F	**Turney**	15-25	N/A	N/A	N/A

Start: Maple Heights, Southgate USA Shopping Center at Libby and Warrensville Center Rd.. *End:* Cleveland, Public Square or E. 13 and Payne. *Trunk route(s):* Turney, Broadway
First bus: 6:44 AM. *Last bus:* 7:24 AM.
First bus, opposite direction: 4:35 PM. *Last bus, opposite direction:* 5:15 PM.
Notes: Three northbound morning buses and three southbound afternoon buses.

77F	**Brecksville**	12	60	90	90

Start: Brecksville, Snowville Rd. (Ameritech). *End:* Cleveland, Public Square. *Trunk route(s):* Brecksville Rd., I-77
First bus: 5:31 AM. *Last bus:* 8:51 PM.
First bus, opposite direction: 6:00 AM. *Last bus, opposite direction:* 9:40 PM.
Notes: This bus makes connections with Akron Metro buses in Brecksville. Limited service to Lombardo Dr. offices and Minoff Industrial Park. Two reverse commute buses in the a.m. and p.m.

78	**West 98 - Puritas**	30-45	50	50	45

Start: Brook Park, NASA at Brookpark and Taylor. *End:* West Blvd. Cudell Red Line Rapid Station. *Trunk route(s):* Puritas, Bellaire, W. 98th
First bus: 4:52 AM. *Last bus:* 10:00 PM.
First bus, opposite direction: 5:38 AM. *Last bus, opposite direction:* 10:45 PM.
Notes: Some buses have a southern terminating stop within NASA's Lewis Research Center at Walcott and Taylor.

79	**Fulton - Ridge**	30-40	30	45	60

Start: North Royalton, Bennett and Ridge or Parma, York and Pleasant Lake. *End:* Cleveland, Public Square. *Trunk route(s):* Ridge, Fulton
First bus: 4:45 AM. *Last bus:* 12:25 AM.
First bus, opposite direction: 4:35 AM. *Last bus, opposite direction:* 12:40 AM.
Notes: Southbound terminus varies by bus and late night buses do not cover entire route. Be sure to check schedule for details. Limited service to Tri-C West Campus.

79X	**Fulton - Ridge**	15	N/A	N/A	N/A

Start: North Royalton, Bennett and Ridge or Parma, York and Pleasant Lake. *End:* Cleveland, Public Square. *Trunk route(s):* Ridge, Fulton, I-71
First bus: 6:19 AM. *Last bus:* 8:03 AM.
First bus, opposite direction: 4:25 PM. *Last bus, opposite direction:* 6:00 PM.
Notes: Southbound terminus varies by bus; be sure to check schedule for details. No service to Tri-C West Campus on this flyer bus.

81	**Tremont - Storer**	20	20	30-60	35-60

Start: Cleveland, West Blvd. Cudell Red Line Rapid Station. *End:* Cleveland, Public Square. *Trunk route(s):* West, Denison, Storer
First bus: 4:30 AM. *Last bus:* 11:29 PM.
First bus, opposite direction: 5:10 AM. *Last bus, opposite direction:* 12:10 AM.
Notes:

83	**West 130**	20-24	25-30	45	45

Start: Parma Heights, West 130th and Pearl (Southland Shopping Center). *End:* Cleveland, Triskett Red Line Rapid Station. *Trunk route(s):* West 130th
First bus: 5:03 AM. *Last bus:* 12:03 AM.
First bus, opposite direction: 4:44 AM. *Last bus, opposite direction:* 10:04 PM.
Notes: Northbound buses before 5:59 AM and after 10:00 PM start route at Brookpark and Chevrolet Blvd. Some southbound buses do not serve southernmost stops.

86	**Warren - Berea**	15-20	42	60	60

Start: Berea, Fair Rd. (and Sprague) Park-n-Ride. *End:* Lakewood, Lakewood Park (Lake Blvd. and Belle). *Trunk route(s):* Prospect, Front, Rocky River, Warren
First bus: 5:25 AM. *Last bus:* 10:07 PM.
First bus, opposite direction: 5:30 AM. *Last bus, opposite direction:* 9:35 PM.
Notes: Some buses continue to or from Drake and Prospect in Strongsville. Limited service before 5:43 AM and after 8:30 PM.

Greater Cleveland RTA Bus and Rapid Routes

Route number	Route name	M-F peak freq.	M-F off-peak freq.	Saturday frequency	Sunday frequency
86F	**Berea - Olmsted Falls**	12-30	N/A	N/A	N/A

Start: Olmsted Falls, Spraque Rd. and Usher OR Berea, Drake and Prospect. *End:* Cleveland, East 18th and Euclid. *Trunk route(s):* I-71
First bus: 5:50 AM. Last bus: 7:24 AM.
First bus, opposite direction: 4:25 PM. Last bus, opposite direction: 6:10 PM.
Notes: 5 northbound morning buses and 6 southbound afternoon buses.

87F	**Westwood - I-90**	20-25	N/A	N/A	N/A

Start: N. Olmsted, Lorain & Dover Center. *End:* Cleveland, East 21st & Euclid. *Trunk route:* I-90
First bus: 6:28 AM. Last bus: 7:35 AM.
First bus, opposite direction: 4:30 PM. Last bus, opposite direction: 5:29 PM.
Notes: Four eastbound morning buses and four westbound afternoon buses.

88X	**Broadway - East 135**	30	40	N/A	N/A

Start: Garfield Heights, Garfield Mall near Rockside and Turney. *End:* Cleveland, East 13th and Payne. *Trunk route(s):* Turney, Broadway
First bus: 5:12 AM. Last bus: 5:25 PM.
First bus, opposite direction: 6:13 AM. Last bus, opposite direction: 6:18 PM.

89	**Southwest Crosstown**	50	60	75	N/A

Start: N. Olmsted, Great N. Mall. *End:* Strongsville, Drake/ Howe. *Trunk route(s):* Bagley, Pearl
First bus: 8:25 AM. Last bus: 6:05 PM.
First bus, opposite direction: 8:40 AM. Last bus, opposite direction: 4:45 PM.
Notes: Serves southwest suburbs of North Olmsted, Olmsted Falls, Berea and Strongsville.

90X	**Broadway - Libby**	15	30	60	60

Start: County Line Loop at Broadway and Richmond. *End:* Cleveland, Prospect and Ontario. *Trunk route(s):* Broadway, Libby
First bus: 5:50 AM. Last bus: 7:48 PM.
First bus, opposite direction: 6:05 AM. Last bus, opposite direction: 8:50 PM.
Notes: Northbound trips travel on Libby. They do not go through Southgate. This bus connects with Akron Metro service at Broadway and Richmond (County Line Loop).

94	**Fairmount - Richmond**	40	40	50	60

Start: Cleveland, University Circle Rapid Station. *End:* Euclid, E.222 and Lakeshore. *Trunk route(s):* Cedar, Fairmount, Richmond, E. 260, Lakeshore
First bus: 4:50 AM. Last bus: 7:30 PM.
First bus, opposite direction: 6:05 AM. Last bus, opposite direction: 7:30 PM.
Notes: First southbound and last two northbound buses have northern terminus at Beachwood Place.

96F	**Butternut - Hilliard**	30	N/A	N/A	N/A

Start: N. Olmsted, Lorain - Dover Ctr. *End:* Cleveland, E. 21 and Euclid Ave. *Trunk route(s):* I-90
First bus: 4:32 PM. Last bus: 5:33 PM.
First bus, opposite direction: 6:24 AM. Last bus, opposite direction: 7:24 AM.
Notes: Three morning buses eastbound and three afternoon buses westbound each weekday.

97F	**Walton Hills**	20	N/A	N/A	N/A

Start: Walton Hills, Alexander & Walton. *End:* Cleveland, E. 13 and Payne. *Trunk route(s):* Northfield, Warrensville, I-480, I- 77
First bus: 6:21 AM. Last bus: 6:49 AM.
First bus, opposite direction: 4:59 PM. Last bus, opposite direction: 5:19 PM.
Notes: Two morning northbound buses and two afternoon southbound buses on weekdays.

97X	**Broadway - Northfield**	35	80	35	N/A

Start: Glen Willow, County Line at Broadway and Richmond. *End:* Cleveland, E. 13 and Payne. *Trunk route(s):* Broadway
First bus: 5:12 AM. Last bus: 5:17 PM.
First bus, opposite direction: 6:14 AM. Last bus, opposite direction: 6:16 PM.
Notes: Also serves Buckthorn and Balsam at limited peak times. RTA proposes route frequency changes for the Fall of 1999.

98	**Brookpark**	60	60	N/A	N/A

Start: Parma, West 33 and Brookpark. *End:* Brookpark, Brookpark Red Line Rapid Station. *Trunk route(s):* Brookpark
First bus: 4:54 AM. Last bus: 5:58 PM.
First bus, opposite direction: 5:25 AM. Last bus, opposite direction: 6:29 PM.

Car-Free in Cleveland

Selected park-n-ride flyer buses

Route number	Route name	M-F peak freq.	M-F off-peak freq.	Saturday frequency	Sunday frequency
239	**Euclid Park & Ride Flyer**	15	N/A	N/A	N/A
	Start: Euclid Park-n-Ride. *End:* Cleveland, Public Sq. *Trunk route(s):* East Shoreway, Babbitt Rd.				
	First bus: 4:00 PM. *Last bus:* 6:15 PM.				
	First bus, opposite direction: 6:15 AM. *Last bus, opposite direction:* 8:30 AM.				
Notes:	Additional service to the Euclid Park & Ride is available on the 1 and 39 bus routes. Also, special event bus service is available from the Euclid Park-n-Ride.				
246	**Westlake Park & Ridge Flyer**	15	N/A	N/A	N/A
	Start: Westlake, Park & Ride. *End:* Cleveland, E. 12th & St. Clair. *Trunk route(s):* I-90				
	First bus: 6:00 AM. *Last bus:* 8:30 AM.				
	First bus, opposite direction: 3:35 PM. *Last bus, opposite direction:* 6:10 PM.				
Notes:	Additional service to the Westlake Park & Ride is available by two evening westbound 55CX trips and by several midday eastbound & westbound 55X trips. Also, special event bus service is available from the Euclid Park-n-Ride.				
251	**I-71/Pearl Rd. Flyer (Park-N-Ride)**	20-45	N/A	N/A	N/A
	Start: Strongsville Park-n-Ride lot. *End:* Cleveland State University (East 22nd and Chester). *Trunk route(s):* I-71				
	First bus: 5:50 AM. *Last bus:* 8:38 AM.				
	First bus, opposite direction: 3:40 PM. *Last bus, opposite direction:* 6:00 PM.				
Notes:	Morning service only northbound and afternoon service only southbound.				
451	**I-71/Pearl Rd. Flyer (Laurel Square)**	15	N/A	N/A	N/A
	Start: Brunswick, Laurel Sq. *End:* Cleveland State Univ (E. 22nd and Chester). *Trunk route:* I-71				
	First bus: 6:10 AM. *Last bus:* 8:04 AM.				
	First bus, opposite direction: 4:20 PM. *Last bus, opposite direction:* 5:50 PM.				
Notes:	Morning service only northbound and afternoon service only southbound.				

Downtown loop buses

147	**Center City Loop**	8	8	N/A	N/A
	Start: Cleveland, E. 18 and Hamilton. *End:* Cleveland, W. 6 and Lakeside. *Trunk route(s):* see map				
	First bus: 5:46 AM. *Last bus:* 6:52 PM.				
	First bus, opposite direction: 6:05 AM. *Last bus, opposite direction:* 7:11 PM.				
Notes:	Route varies between Euclid and Superior -- see map				
247	**Outer Loop**	8	8	N/A	N/A
	Start: Cleveland, Municipal Parking Lot at E. 9 and South Marginal. *End:* Cleveland, E. 30 and Community College Ave.. *Trunk route(s):* see map				
	First bus: 6:28 AM. *Last bus:* 6:28 PM.				
	First bus, opposite direction: 5:30 AM. *Last bus, opposite direction:* 6:00 PM.				
Notes:	Route varies between E 21 and E 30 -- see map				

Special attractions buses

441	**Geauga Lake/Sea World**	30	30	30	30
	Start: Aurora, theme parks. *End:* Shaker Hts., Warrensville Rapid station (Blue Line). *Trunk route(s):* Warrensville, Libby, Aurora				
	First bus: 6:50 AM. *Last bus:* 10:48 PM.				
	First bus, opposite direction: 7:55 AM. *Last bus, opposite direction:* 11:55 PM.				
Notes:	Operates only when Sea World and Geauga Lake theme parks are open, typically from May to September. Late evening service only available in peak season.				
20C	**Metroparks Zoo**	N/A	60	60	60
	Start: Cleveland, Superior and West Roadway. *End:* Cleveland, Metroparks Zoo. *Trunk route:* W. 25				
	First bus: 10:00 AM. *Last bus:* 4:30 PM.				
	First bus, opposite direction: 9:30 AM. *Last bus, opposite direction:* 5:05 PM.				
Notes:	Services operates on many holidays/all buses are lift equipped				

Greater Cleveland RTA Bus and Rapid Routes

Community circulator buses

Route number	Route name	M-F peak freq.	M-F off-peak freq.	Saturday frequency	Sunday frequency
801	Lee - Harvard Community Circulator	30	30	30	N/A

Start and End: Cleveland, Corlett and E. 130 bus loop.
First bus: 6:02 AM. *Last bus:* 6:33 PM.
First bus, opposite direction: 5:58 AM. *Last bus, opposite direction:* 6:29 PM.
Notes: Serves the Lee-Harvard neighborhood of southeast Cleveland and the Onaway Station of RTA's Blue Line in Shaker Heights. Saturday service from 6:08 AM to 6:33 PM.

802	Southeast Community Circulator	20	20	20	N/A

Start and End: Maple Heights, Broadway and Libby.
First bus: 6:00 AM. *Last bus:* 7:00 PM.
First bus, opposite direction: 6:00 AM. *Last bus, opposite direction:* 7:00 PM.
Notes: Serves shopping centers in the southeast suburbs of Warrensville Heights, Maple Heights, and North Randall.

803	St. Clair Community Circulator	20	20	20	N/A

Start and End: Cleveland, E. 55 and St. Clair.
First bus: 6:00 AM. *Last bus:* 7:00 PM.
First bus, opposite direction: 6:00 AM. *Last bus, opposite direction:* 7:00 PM.
Notes: Serves the St. Clair and Hough neighborhoods of Cleveland between E. 30th and E. 89th.

804	Lakewood Community Circulator	20	20	30	N/A

Start and End: Lakewood, West 117 Red Line Rapid Station.
First bus: 6:00 AM. *Last bus:* 7:00 PM.
First bus, opposite direction: 6:00 AM. *Last bus, opposite direction:* 7:00 PM.
Notes: Serves Lakewood between the W. 117th St. Rapid Station and the Rocky River Loop. Saturday service from 8:00 AM to 6:00 PM.

805	Slavic Village Community Circulator	15	15	20	30

Start: Cuyahoga Hts., Village Hall at E. 71 and Dressler. *End:* Cleveland, E. 65 and Broadway.
First bus: 6:00 AM. *Last bus:* 10:35 PM.
First bus, opposite direction: 6:18 AM. *Last bus, opposite direction:* 11:13 PM.
Notes: Serves the Broadway - Slavic Village neighborhoods of Cleveland and Cuyahoga Heights. Saturday service from 7:00 AM to 10:00 PM. Sunday service from 8:00 AM to 8:00 PM.

806	Euclid Community Circulator	15	15	15	N/A

Start: Euclid, Lake Shore and E. 185. *End:* Euclid, Euclid Blvd. and E. 276.
First bus: 6:03 AM. *Last bus:* 7:03 PM.
First bus, opposite direction: 6:00 AM. *Last bus, opposite direction:* 7:00 PM.
Notes: Serves the city of Euclid between Euclid Meridia Hospital and Euclid Blvd. and E. 276th.

807	Tremont Community Circulator	20	20	30	30

Start: Cleveland, Dennison near Ridge. *End:* Cleveland, Lakeview Terrace on Washington near W. 25. *Trunk route(s):* see map
First bus: 6:00 AM. *Last bus:* 7:10 PM.
First bus, opposite direction: 6:00 AM. *Last bus, opposite direction:* 7:00 PM.
Notes: Serves the Tremont neighborhood on Cleveland's west side. Saturday/ Sunday service from 8:00 AM to 6:00 PM.

808	Westshore Community Circulator	20	20	30	N/A

Start and End: Westgate Transit Center in Fairview Park.
First bus: 6:00 AM. *Last bus:* 8:00 PM.
First bus, opposite direction: 6:00 AM. *Last bus, opposite direction:* 8:00 PM.
Notes: Serves the cities of Fairview Park, Westlake and Rocky River. Saturday service from 10:00 AM to 6:00 PM. No Sunday service.

Car-Free in Cleveland

Alternative Transportation
Cleveland

Alt Trans Cleveland is a new group advocating sustainable neighborhoods through the promotion of a balanced, coordinated transportation system for Northeast Ohio.

You have in your hands the results of our first effort...*Car-Free in Cleveland*. We are the only alternative transportation advocacy organization in Northeast Ohio. If you'd like updates on the work we are doing just clip out the form below and send it in to EcoCity Cleveland, 2841 Scarborough Rd., Cleveland Heights OH 44118.

Name _____
Address _____
City _____**State** _____**Zip** _____
Phone _____
e-mail _____
Comments _____

For more information, please call 216-932-3007 or visit the EcoCity Cleveland Web site at www.ecocleveland.org.

Car-Free in Cleveland

EcoCity Cleveland

EcoCity Cleveland is a nonprofit environmental planning organization that promotes a vision of ecological cities existing in balance with their surrounding countryside. We publish an award-winning journal that reports on the environmental and urban issues shaping the future of Northeast Ohio. Our *Citizens' Bioregional Plan* has mapped out more sustainable patterns of development in the region. Our *Ohio Smart Growth Agenda* has proposed growth management reforms for the state. And our Cleveland EcoVillage project is demonstrating how urban neighborhoods can be revitalized with the best ecological designs. In addition, our 340-page guide, *The Greater Cleveland Environment Book*, is the owner's manual for everyone who wants to take better care of Northeast Ohio.

You can join EcoCity Cleveland by subscribing to our journal. Other publications are also available by filling out the coupon below.

For more information, call us at 216-932-3007, or see our Web site at www.ecocleveland.org.

SUBSCRIBE NOW!

EcoCity Cleveland will bring you the ideas and information you need to create a more sustainable bioregion in Northeast Ohio.

Name _____
Address _____
City _____ State _____ Zip _____
Bioregion _____
Telephone _____

- ❏ New or ❏ renewal regular one-year journal subscription – $20.
- ❏ Supporting journal subscription – $35 or more.
- ❏ The Greater Cleveland Environment Book – $19.
- ❏ Citizen's Bioregional Plan – $5.
- ❏ Ohio Smart Growth Agenda – $4.
    (all prices include tax and shipping)

Please make checks payable to EcoCity Cleveland and send to
2841 Scarborough Rd., Cleveland Heights, OH 44118.

Car-Free® in Boston

Car-Free® in Boston is the original "Car-Free®" guide to transit and other auto-free ways to get around. Make sure to pick up a copy next time you're in Boston. For more information contact:

Car-Free® in Boston/ APT, at P.O. Box 1029, Boston, MA 02205 or call 617-482-0282.

The Association for Public Transportation is a nonprofit organization that, in addition to publishing *Car-Free® in Boston*, has worked for over 20 years to improve Boston's public transit for the benefit of both the rider and the environment.

Car-Free in Cleveland

Breathe easy.

Ride RTA

RTA buses and rapid transits greatly reduce automobile traffic. And fewer cars on the roads means less pollution and cleaner air.

RTA helps improve our air quality and actually saves RTA riders money. Around $84 million a year that would otherwise be spent on gas, parking and car maintenance.

Now you can save, too. Use the coupon below to save one dollar on your next RTA weekly pass. It's not $84 million, but it's a start. Start breathing easier. Ride RTA.

Save $1 Present this coupon for 1$ off the price of any express or weekly pass. Redeemable only at RTA Customer Service Center located in the BP Building at 315 Euclid Avenue. This offer is not valid with any other offer or discount. Offer expires June 1, 2001. **Save $1**

105

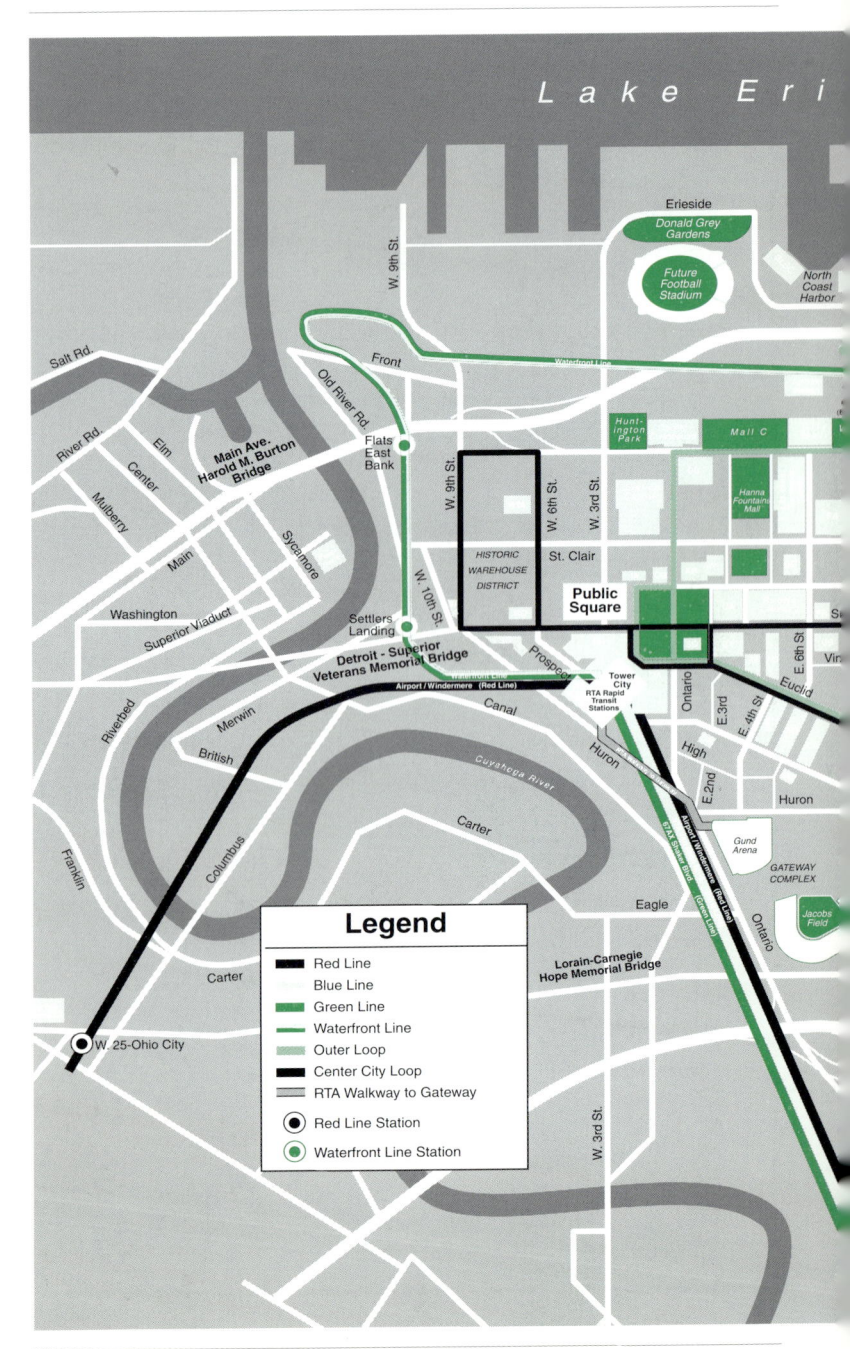

Car-Free in Cleveland

Car-Free in Cleveland

107

Car-Free in Cleveland

GET INVOLVED!

By now you know that being car-free in Cleveland is easier than most people think. We Northeast Ohioans have lots of good options for getting around the region by transit, bike, and on foot.

But we're still a long way from being a truly great car-free region. If you want to get involved in making lower-mileage living more viable for everyone, there's a lot you can do:

➪ Join Alt-Trans Cleveland! Look for our membership application at the back of this book. We're a new group and your membership and involvement can make a big difference.

➪ Learn more about transportation decision-making in Northeast Ohio by attending NOACA meetings. The Northeast Ohio Areawide Coordinating Agency is Greater Cleveland's metro transportation planning organization. There are plenty of opportunities for you to make your voice heard. Call NOACA at 216-241-2414 or see www.noaca.org to get more information.

➪ Get involved with decision-making at RTA or your local transit agency. Bus routes and schedule changes, new investments and ridership policy revisions are never made without involving the public. Call your transit agency for more information.

➪ Let your mayor, council representative or township trustees know that you support good transportation choices and tell them what you'd like to see done. Call or write them today.

➪ Follow issues at your local planning commission and zoning boards. Transit and pedestrian-unfriendly decisions are made every day because no one speaks out.

➪ Read the *EcoCity Cleveland Journal* to learn more about creating sustainable, transit-friendly communities in Northeast Ohio. Call 216-932-3007 for a free sample copy. Also, subscribe to "Getting Where We Want To Be", the free fax and e-mail bulletin for transportation policy news from EcoCity Cleveland.

➪ Join one of the many other nonprofit organizations that are involved in making Greater Cleveland a better place for pedestrians, bicyclists and transit riders - groups like the Cleveland Waterfront Coalition, the Sierra Club, the Committee for Public Art, and the Earth Day Coalition. Also, religious institutions care deeply about their neighborhoods and many are actively working to make them better places for everyone, including the car-free. Making a difference is always easier in numbers.

➪ When you're thinking about moving your household, pick a neighborhood where living without car dependency is an option.

➪ Walk the talk! The more we use transit, the better service they can offer. The more we bicycle, the more motorists will learn to share the road. The more we walk, the more likely we will see streets and communities designed with pedestrian safety, convenience and enjoyment in mind.